The PowerPoint Edge - Mastering the Art of Storytelling

The PowerPoint Edge - Mastering the Art of Storytelling

Table of Contents

About the Author:

Santosh Cholle writes book, which, considering while you're reading this, makes a perfect sense.

Born in Mumbai, began writing in 2022 and has contributed to his debut book 'The Excel Edge'. 'The Derivatives Edge' and ' The PowerPoint Edge' is his third book.

His work across multiple disciplines broadly addresses nuances of Personal Finance, MS Office & Technology.

He holds a Master's in Business Administration degree from IIMM Pune and a Bachelor's degree in Arts from the University of Mumbai.

He currently lives with his wife and family in Pune and loves travelling across the globe.

Also by Santosh Cholle

The Excel Edge -
Mastering Spreadsheets for Business and Beyond

The Derivatives Edge -
Taming the Wild Beast of Finance

To my Son

&

My Wife

The PowerPoint Edge

Mastering the Art of Storytelling

Santosh Cholle

1

Introduction to PowerPoint Presentations

The PowerPoint Edge - Mastering the Art of Storytelling

PowerPoint is fun, I learnt it while I was doing my Masters in Software Engineering at Aptech. Right out from Indian Airforce it was fun doing MS office. I was already working with Windows** during my Airforce career, when it was introduced as a full-fledged version in the year 1995.

**(*Microsoft Windows was first introduced on November 20, 1985. The initial version, Windows 1.0, was a graphical operating system shell for MS-DOS, and it was designed to make it easier for users to navigate their computers using a mouse and keyboard. Since then, Microsoft has released numerous versions of Windows, including Windows 95, Windows XP, Windows 7, Windows 10, and most recently, Windows 11. Windows has become one of the most widely used operating systems in the world, powering millions of personal computers and devices worldwide*)

I was posted in Electronics Data Processing Wing (EDPw) in Indian Airforce in New Delhi. Starting with data entry initially, I had started doing programming in COBOL, the most used programming language then. I also had hands on experience on working with MS-DOS, UNIX, SHELL, Excel and Word while in my Indian Airforce career. I was the top-performing student in the first two semesters after I joined Aptech. I also used to conduct classes at times for fellow mates during the absence of the Aptech faculty. However, I later lost interest as whatever was taught in that institute, I already had mastered in it during my Airforce career.

With regards to my teaching experiences, high ranking officers from Army, Navy, BSF were my initial students. Since Indian Airforce being the first wing to have acquired computers and we – a group of 20 programmers had this responsibility to train officers of other wings. It was fun and an enriching experience, sitting beside them and make them to key in basic commands in DOS like 'Dir', 'Cd', etc.

Began teaching 'computers' to say from Indian Airforce, then in Aptech Institute. Conducted tuitions at home, sessions during weekends at Orphanages in Mumbai & Pune, conducted several sessions for the employees at – 'The Thriarr Polymers', 'The Wallace floor mills', 'Vodafone', 'Sitel India', 'IBM, Citigroup, Tech Mahindra, TCS.

Now, into writing, my first book being 'The Excel Edge' on basics to advanced excel, Second book 'The Derivatives Edge' on Derivatives trading and third is this 'The Powerpoint Edge'.

Getting on to the subject – PowerPoint in a gist is nothing but telling your story in a most presentable manner. How to make it 'well-dressed' and more presentable are discussed in the chapters to come.

First, let's understand how PowerPoint evolved.

PowerPoint was invented by Robert Gaskins and Dennis Austin in 1984 while they were working at a software company called Forethought, Inc. The initial version of PowerPoint was called "Presenter" and was designed for the Apple Macintosh computer. Later, Microsoft acquired PowerPoint and integrated it into their Office suite of applications. Today, PowerPoint is one of the most widely used presentation software programs in the world.

PowerPoint is a powerful tool and it has been an essential part of business and education ever since. PowerPoint presentations are a way of communicating information visually, and they can be used for a variety of purposes, such as presenting new ideas, training employees, and selling products.

In this book, we will explore how to create effective PowerPoint presentations that engage and inform your audience. We will cover the basics of PowerPoint, including how to choose the right layout, how to use graphics and charts, and how to deliver a successful presentation.

PowerPoint presentations are a common tool used in business, education, and other settings to convey information in a visually appealing and organized manner. They can be used to present new ideas, to train employees, to report on research findings, and to sell products or services. Here are a few examples of how PowerPoint presentations are used in different contexts:

Business Presentations:

In the business world, PowerPoint presentations are often used to present information to colleagues, clients, and investors. For example, a sales representative might use a PowerPoint presentation to showcase the features and benefits of a new product to a potential customer. Or a CEO might use a PowerPoint presentation to provide an overview of the company's financial performance to investors.

Business presentations are an essential part of corporate communication, whether it's to share company updates, showcase a new product, or present a proposal to potential investors. Here are some tips for creating effective business presentations using PowerPoint:

- **Start with a clear objective:** Define the purpose of your presentation and determine what you want your audience to take away from it. This will help you structure your presentation and focus on the most important points.

- **Know your audience:** Understand your audience's needs, expectations, and level of knowledge to tailor your presentation accordingly. This will help you present your message in a way that is relevant and engaging to your audience.

- **Use visuals effectively:** Use visuals, such as charts, graphs, and images, to support your message and make it easier for your audience to understand complex information. Keep your visuals simple and easy to read, and use them to highlight key points.

- **Keep it concise:** Business presentations should be clear, concise, and to the point. Avoid using jargon or technical language that your audience may not understand, and keep your presentation focused on your main message.

- **Tell a story:** Use storytelling techniques to engage your audience and make your presentation more memorable. Incorporate anecdotes, case studies, or real-world examples to bring your message to life.

- **Use a professional design:** Use a professional design that aligns with your company's branding and reflects the tone and style of your presentation. Use colours, fonts, and graphics that are easy on the eyes and create a cohesive look and feel.

- **Practice your delivery:** Practice your delivery to become comfortable with the material and the flow of the presentation. Rehearse your presentation in front of colleagues or friends to receive feedback and make any necessary adjustments.

- **End with a call to action:** End your presentation with a clear call to action that encourages your audience to take the next step, whether it's to sign up for a service, make a purchase, or contact your company for more information.

By following these tips, you can create effective business presentations using PowerPoint that engage your audience and effectively communicate your message.

Educational Presentations:

In education, PowerPoint presentations are frequently used to teach new concepts and provide visual aids for students. For example, a science teacher might use a PowerPoint presentation to explain the different stages of photosynthesis, using diagrams and images to make the process easier to understand. Similarly, a history teacher might use a PowerPoint presentation to show images of important events and historical figures during a lecture.

Educational presentations in PowerPoint are an effective way to engage students and facilitate learning. Here are some tips for creating effective educational presentations:

- **Define the learning objectives**: of your presentation and determine what you want your students to take away from it. This will help you structure your presentation and focus on the most important points.

- **Effective visuals:** Use visuals, such as images, videos, and animations, to support your message and make it easier for students to understand complex information. Keep your visuals simple and easy to read, and use them to highlight key points.

- **Keep it simple:** Educational presentations should be clear, concise, and to the point. Avoid using jargon or technical language that your students may not understand, and keep your presentation focused on the most important concepts.

- **Use interactive features:** Use interactive features, such as quizzes, polls, and interactive games, to engage students and reinforce their learning. This can help keep students interested and make learning more enjoyable.

- **Provide context:** Provide context for the information you are presenting and help students understand how it fits into the bigger picture. Use real-world examples or case studies to help students see the practical applications of the information they are learning.

- **Use a consistent design:** Use a consistent design that aligns with your educational institution's branding and reflects the tone and style of your presentation. Use colours, fonts, and graphics that are easy on the eyes and create a cohesive look and feel.

- **Use storytelling**: Use storytelling techniques to engage your students and make your presentation more memorable. Incorporate anecdotes, case studies, or real-world examples to bring your message to life.

- **Practice your delivery:** Practice your delivery to become comfortable with the material and the flow of the presentation. Rehearse your presentation in front of colleagues or friends to receive feedback and make any necessary adjustments.

By following these tips, you can create effective educational presentations using PowerPoint that engage your students and facilitate learning.

Research Presentations:

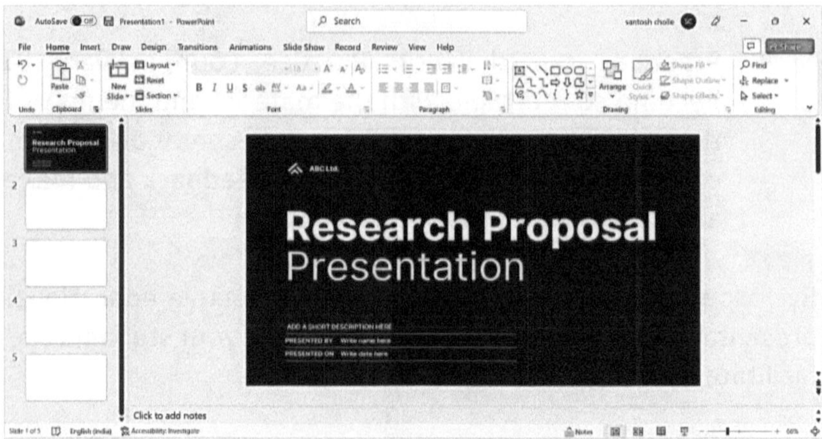

In academic and scientific settings, PowerPoint presentations are often used to present research findings to colleagues and peers. For example, a researcher might use a PowerPoint presentation to present the results of a study at a conference, using tables, charts, and graphs to display the data.

Research presentations in PowerPoint are commonly used to showcase the results of a study or experiment. Here are some tips for creating effective research presentations:

- **Start with a clear objective:** Define the research objective and the key findings you want to present. Determine what message you want to communicate to your audience and structure your presentation around that message.

- **Use visuals effectively:** Use charts, graphs, and other visual aids to present your research findings. Keep your visuals simple and easy to read, and use them to highlight key data points.

- **Organize your data logically**: Organize your data in a logical manner to make it easy for your audience to follow along. Use headings and subheadings to structure your presentation and guide your audience through the key findings.

- **Be clear and concise:** Research presentations should be clear and concise, with a focus on the most important findings. Avoid using technical jargon or complex language that may be difficult for your audience to understand.

- **Use citations:** Use citations to give credit to the sources you used in your research. This not only helps you avoid plagiarism but also adds credibility to your presentation.

- **Provide context:** Provide context for your research findings by discussing the broader implications and how they fit into the larger body of research in your field. This helps your audience understand the significance of your findings.

- **Practice your delivery:** Practice your delivery to become comfortable with the material and the flow of the presentation. Rehearse your presentation in front of colleagues or friends to receive feedback and make any necessary adjustments.

By following these tips, you can create effective research presentations using PowerPoint that effectively communicate your findings and their significance to your audience.

Marketing Presentations:

In marketing, PowerPoint presentations can be used to create visual presentations that showcase products or services to potential customers. For example, a marketing team might use a PowerPoint presentation to pitch a new advertising campaign to a client, using images, videos, and statistics to show the potential effectiveness of the campaign.

In all of these contexts, PowerPoint presentations are used to communicate information in a clear and visually appealing way, making it easier for the audience to understand and remember the key points being presented.

Marketing presentations in PowerPoint are often used to promote a product, service, or brand. Here are some tips for creating effective marketing presentations:

- **Know your audience**: Understanding your target audience is essential to creating a successful marketing presentation. Consider their interests, preferences, and pain points when developing your presentation.

- **Define your message:** Clearly define your marketing message and focus on the key benefits of your product or service. Keep your presentation focused on the most important information and avoid overwhelming your audience with too much detail.

- **Use visuals effectively:** Use visuals, such as images, videos, and infographics, to support your message and make it more engaging. Use high-quality images and graphics that align with your brand's style and messaging.

- **Be creative:** Use creative and innovative approaches to capture your audience's attention and keep them engaged throughout your presentation. Consider using storytelling techniques, interactive elements, or unique visuals to make your presentation stand out.

- **Keep it simple:** Keep your presentation simple and easy to follow. Use clear and concise language that your audience can easily understand, and avoid technical jargon or industry-specific terms.

- **Use social proof:** Incorporate social proof, such as customer testimonials or case studies, to build trust and credibility with your audience. This can help convince them to take action and make a purchase.

- **End with a call to action:** End your presentation with a clear call to action that encourages your audience to take the desired action, such as making a purchase or signing up for a service.

- **Practice your delivery:** Practice your delivery to become comfortable with the material and the flow of the presentation. Rehearse your presentation in front of colleagues or friends to receive feedback and make any necessary adjustments.

By following these tips, you can create effective marketing presentations using PowerPoint that effectively promote your product, service, or brand to your target audience.

Understanding 'The workspace' in Powerpoint

PowerPoint is one of the most widely used presentation software in the world, and it has a workspace that is specifically designed to help users create engaging and informative presentations. Understanding the workspace in PowerPoint is essential for anyone who wants to create professional-looking presentations that effectively communicate their message. In this segment, we will explore the PowerPoint workspace and discuss its various elements and their functions.

Slide Area:

The slide area is the main part of the PowerPoint workspace, where you create your presentation's content. This is where you can add text, images, charts, tables, videos, and other multimedia elements. The slide area is the space where you can get creative with your presentation and design slides that effectively communicate your message.

Slides Pane:

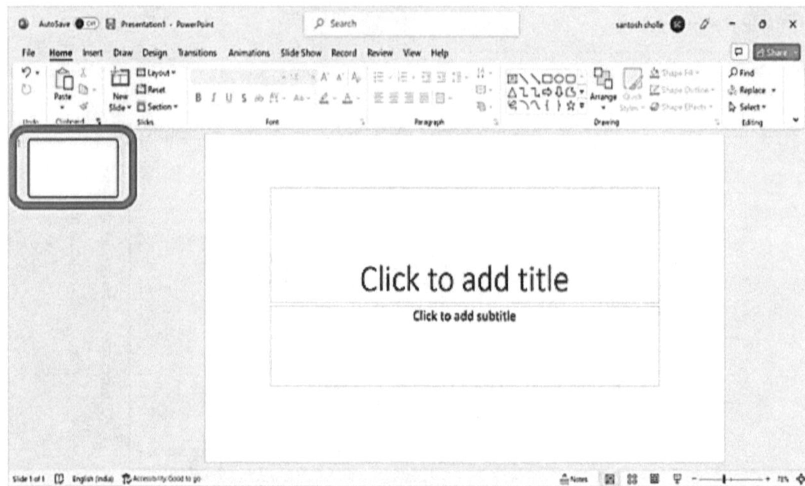

The slides pane is the section of the workspace where you can see a thumbnail view of all the slides in your presentation. The slide pane is located on the left-hand side of the screen and allows you to navigate quickly between different slides. You can also use the slide pane to rearrange the order of your slides or delete them.

Notes Pane:

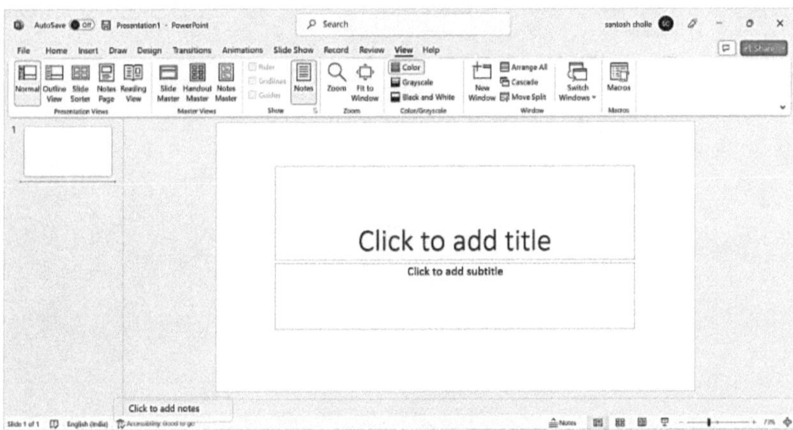

The notes pane is located at the bottom of the PowerPoint workspace, and it allows you to add speaker notes to your presentation. These notes can be helpful during a presentation as they can remind you of key points, statistics, or other information that you want to convey. Speaker notes can be added to each slide individually, and you can print them out as a reference for your presentation.

The PowerPoint Edge - Mastering the Art of Storytelling

Ribbon:

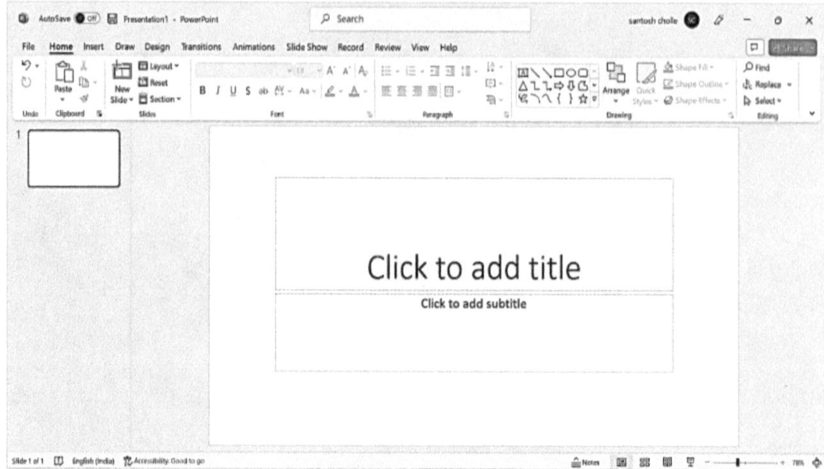

The ribbon is located at the top of the PowerPoint workspace, and it contains all the tools and features you need to create your presentation. The ribbon is divided into several tabs, each with its own set of tools. The tabs include Home, Insert, Design, Transitions, Animations, Slide Show, Review, and View. You can customize the ribbon to add or remove tools based on your preferences.

Quick Access Toolbar:

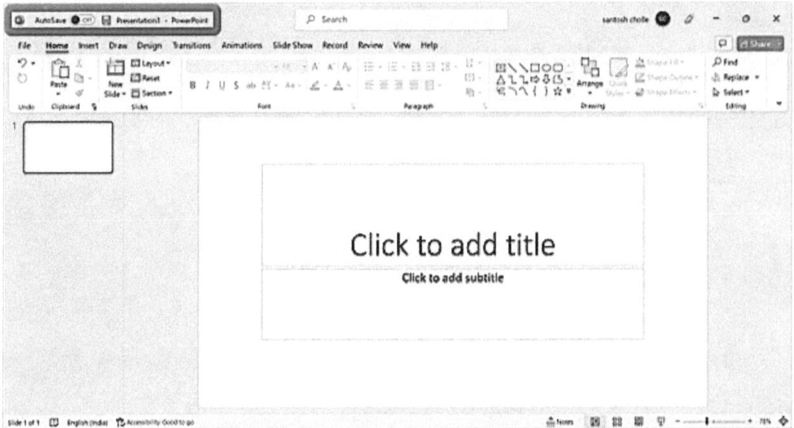

The quick access toolbar is located above the ribbon and allows you to access frequently used tools quickly. You can customize the quick access toolbar to include the tools that you use the most. By default, the quick access toolbar contains buttons for Save, Undo, and Redo.

Status Bar:

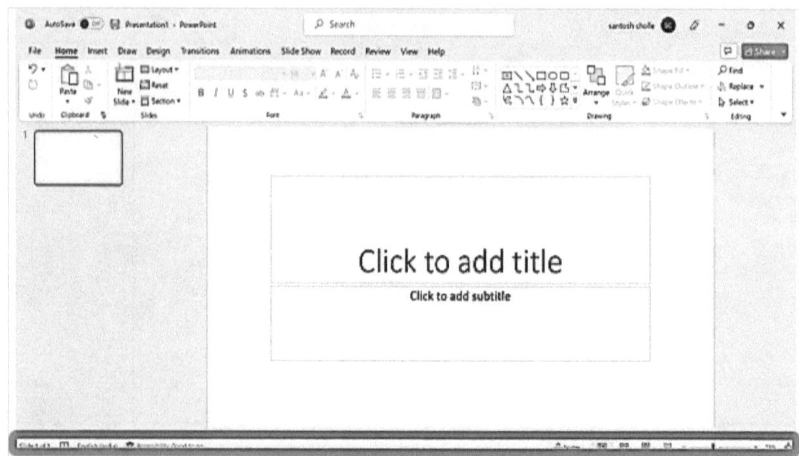

The status bar is located at the bottom of the PowerPoint workspace, and it displays information about the current slide and the status of the presentation. The status bar includes information such as the slide number, the view you are currently in, the zoom level, and the current slide's design.

Conclusion:

In conclusion, the PowerPoint workspace is a comprehensive platform designed to help users create visually appealing and informative presentations. By understanding the various elements of the PowerPoint workspace, you can create presentations that effectively communicate your message and engage your audience. Whether you're a beginner or an experienced PowerPoint user, mastering the workspace's different features can help you create engaging presentations that are sure to impress.

2

Understanding Your Audience

The key to creating an effective PowerPoint presentation is to understand your audience. You need to know who they are, what they want to learn, and what their level of expertise is. By tailoring your presentation to your audience, you can ensure that they will be engaged and interested in what you have to say.

In this chapter, we will explore how to research your audience, how to analyse their needs and expectations, and how to use this information to create a presentation that speaks directly to them.

Understanding your audience is a critical aspect of creating effective PowerPoint presentations. Without a clear understanding of your audience, it can be difficult to create a presentation that effectively communicates your message and engages your audience. Here are some tips for understanding your audience when creating PowerPoint presentations:

- **Demographics:** Consider the age, gender, education level, profession, and cultural background of your audience. This can help you tailor your presentation to better resonate with their values and interests.

- **Knowledge level:** Assess your audience's level of knowledge on the topic you are presenting. Are they experts in the field or newcomers to the topic? This can help you determine the level of detail you need to provide in your presentation.

- **Interests:** Determine what interests your audience and what they hope to gain from your presentation.

Understanding their motivations can help you create content that is relevant and engaging.

- **Expectations:** Identify your audience's expectations for your presentation. Are they expecting to be entertained, educated, or persuaded? Knowing this can help you tailor your approach and make sure you meet their expectations.

- **Communication preferences:** Consider how your audience prefers to receive information. Do they respond better to visual aids, such as charts and diagrams, or do they prefer to listen to a more narrative presentation? This can help you structure your presentation in a way that resonates with your audience.

By taking the time to understand your audience, you can create a PowerPoint presentation that speaks directly to their needs and interests. This can help you build trust and credibility, engage your audience, and ultimately achieve your desired outcomes.

Identify your audience:

The first step in understanding your audience is to identify who they are. Consider their age, gender, education level, profession, and any other relevant factors that may impact how they receive and interpret your presentation.

Identifying your audience is a crucial first step in creating an effective PowerPoint presentation. Here are some key factors to consider when identifying your audience:

- **Demographics:** Consider the age, gender, education level, and other demographic characteristics of your audience. This can help you tailor your presentation to their needs and interests.

- **Knowledge level:** Consider the level of knowledge your audience has on the topic you will be presenting. If they are unfamiliar with the subject matter, you may need to provide more background information and definitions.

- **Purpose:** Consider the purpose of your presentation and what you want to achieve. Are you trying to persuade, inform, or entertain your audience? This can help you determine the tone and content of your presentation.

- **Attitudes and beliefs**: Consider the attitudes and beliefs of your audience toward the topic. This can help you anticipate potential objections or questions and prepare responses accordingly.

- **Context:** Consider the context in which your presentation will be delivered. Will it be a formal business presentation, a classroom lecture, or an informal gathering? This can help you tailor your presentation to the appropriate level of formality and engagement.

Once you have identified your audience, you can use this information to tailor your PowerPoint presentation to their needs and interests. This can help you create a more engaging and effective presentation that resonates with your audience and achieves your goals.

Determine their needs:

Once you've identified your audience, consider their needs and what they hope to gain from your presentation. What are their pain points or challenges? What information do they need to make a decision or take action? By understanding their needs, you can tailor your presentation to effectively address them.

After identifying your audience, the next step in creating an effective PowerPoint presentation is to determine their needs. Understanding your audience's needs can help you tailor your presentation to provide value and address their concerns. Here are some tips for determining your audience's needs:

- **Conduct research:** Conduct research to gather information about your audience's needs and preferences. This can include online surveys, focus groups, or interviews with individuals in your target audience.

- **Analyse existing data:** Analyse existing data to gain insights into your audience's behaviour and preferences. This can include website analytics, customer feedback, or industry research.

- **Consider the context**: Consider the context in which your presentation will be delivered and the goals you want to achieve. This can help you identify the specific needs of your audience and how your presentation can meet those needs.

- **Identify pain points:** Identify the pain points and challenges that your audience is facing and address them in your presentation. This can help you provide value and position your presentation as a solution to their problems.

- **Use empathy:** Use empathy to put yourself in your audience's shoes and understand their perspective. This can help you create a presentation that is more relatable and resonates with your audience.

By determining your audience's needs, you can create a PowerPoint presentation that is relevant, engaging, and meets their specific needs. This can help you build credibility, establish trust, and achieve your goals.

Consider their level of expertise:

Consider your audience's level of expertise on the topic you're presenting. Are they experts in the field, or are they new to the subject? This will impact the level of detail and complexity you should include in your presentation.

When creating a PowerPoint presentation, it's important to consider the level of expertise of your audience. This will help you choose appropriate language, examples, and visuals to ensure that your message is understood and well-received. Here are some tips for considering your audience's level of expertise:

- **Identify the level of expertise:** Determine the level of expertise of your audience by considering their educational background, job title, and experience in the industry. This will help you understand how much technical jargon you can use and how much detail you need to provide.

- **Use appropriate language:** Use language that your audience will understand. Avoid using technical jargon or acronyms that may not be familiar to them. If you need to use technical terms, be sure to define them clearly.

- **Choose appropriate visuals:** Choose visuals that are appropriate for your audience's level of expertise. If your audience is highly technical, you may be able to use complex charts and graphs. If your audience is less technical, you may need to use simpler visuals to illustrate your points.

- **Provide context:** Provide context for your information to help your audience understand how it fits into the bigger picture. This can help them see the relevance of the information and how it can be applied in their work.

- **Test your presentation:** Test your presentation with individuals who have a similar level of expertise to your audience. This can help you identify any areas where you may need to adjust your language, visuals, or content to better suit your audience's needs.

By considering your audience's level of expertise, you can create a PowerPoint presentation that is more engaging, relevant, and effective. This can help you build credibility and establish trust with your audience, and ultimately achieve your goals.

Use appropriate language:

The language you use in your presentation should be appropriate for your audience. Avoid technical jargon and complex terms if your audience is not familiar with them. On the other hand, if your audience is composed of experts, you may need to use more technical language to effectively communicate your message.

Using appropriate language in your PowerPoint presentation is essential for ensuring that your message is clear and easily understood by your audience. Here are some tips for using appropriate language:

- **Use clear and concise language:** Use clear and concise language that is easy to understand. Avoid using jargon or technical terms that your audience may not be familiar with.

- **Define technical terms**: If you need to use technical terms, define them clearly so that your audience can understand them.

- **Avoid filler words:** Avoid using filler words such as "um" or "ah." These can be distracting and make your presentation less effective.

- **Use active voice:** Use active voice instead of passive voice. Active voice is more engaging and helps to keep your audience interested.

- **Use appropriate tone:** Use an appropriate tone for your audience and the subject matter. If you're presenting to a professional audience, use a professional tone. If you're presenting to a more casual audience, you can use a more conversational tone.

- **Use visual aids:** Use visual aids such as images, graphs, or charts to illustrate your points. This can help to break up the text and make your presentation more engaging.

- **Use examples:** Use examples to help illustrate your points and make them more relatable to your audience.

By using appropriate language in your PowerPoint presentation, you can make it more engaging, understandable, and effective. It will also help you to build credibility and establish trust with your audience, which can ultimately help you to achieve your goals.

Address their concerns:

Consider any potential concerns or objections your audience may have about your message. Address these concerns in your presentation to help build trust and credibility with your audience

When creating a PowerPoint presentation, it's important to address the concerns of your audience. By doing so, you can build trust and credibility with them and make your presentation more effective. Here are some tips for addressing your audience's concerns:

- **Understand your audience's perspective**: Before you start creating your presentation, it's important to understand your audience's perspective. Consider their interests, concerns, and motivations.

- **Address common concerns:** Consider the common concerns or objections your audience might have and address them in your presentation. This can help to build trust and credibility with your audience.

- **Use case studies or examples:** Use case studies or examples to show how others have addressed similar concerns or objections. This can help to reassure your audience and build trust.

- **Be transparent:** Be transparent about any potential drawbacks or risks associated with your proposal or recommendation. This shows that you are being honest and upfront with your audience.

- **Use data:** Use data to support your points and address concerns. This can help to build credibility and make your presentation more persuasive.

- **Provide solutions:** Provide solutions to address your audience's concerns. This shows that you have considered their needs and are providing practical solutions.

By addressing the concerns of your audience in your PowerPoint presentation, you can build trust and credibility with them and make your presentation more effective. This can ultimately help you to achieve your goals and objectives.

Use relevant examples:

Examples and case studies can be effective tools in engaging your audience and helping them understand your message. Use examples that are relevant to your audience and demonstrate the value of your message.

Using relevant examples in your PowerPoint presentation can help to illustrate your points and make them more understandable and relatable to your audience. Here are some tips for using relevant examples in your presentation:

- **Choose examples that are relevant to your audience:** Make sure that the examples you use are relevant to your audience and their interests. This can help to keep them engaged and interested in your presentation.

- **Use real-life examples:** Use real-life examples that your audience can relate to. This can help to make your presentation more engaging and memorable.

- **Use examples to illustrate your points:** Use examples to help illustrate your points and make them more understandable to your audience. This can help to clarify complex ideas and make your presentation more effective.

- **Use examples to show the benefits:** Use examples to show the benefits of your proposal or recommendation. This can help to persuade your audience and make them more likely to take action.

- **Use data to support your examples:** Use data to support your examples and make them more credible. This can help to build trust and make your presentation more persuasive.

- **Use visuals to illustrate your examples:** Use visuals such as images, charts, or graphs to illustrate your examples. This can help to make your presentation more engaging and memorable.

By using relevant examples in your PowerPoint presentation, you can make it more engaging and effective. It can also help you to build credibility and establish trust with your audience, which can ultimately help you to achieve your goals.

Overall, understanding your audience is a critical component of creating effective PowerPoint presentations. By taking the time to identify their needs and concerns, and tailoring your message to effectively address them, you can create presentations that effectively communicate your message and engage your audience.

3

Planning Your Presentation

Before you begin creating your PowerPoint presentation, you need to plan it out. This includes determining the purpose of your presentation, organizing your content, and creating an outline.

In this chapter, we will explore the different types of PowerPoint presentations, how to create an effective outline, and how to organize your content in a way that is easy for your audience to follow.

Planning is a crucial step in creating effective PowerPoint presentations. By planning your presentation, you can ensure that your message is clear, your content is well-organized, and your visuals are engaging. Here are some tips for planning your presentation in PowerPoint:

Define your purpose:

The first step in planning your presentation is to define your purpose. What message do you want to convey? What are your goals for the presentation? Answering these questions will help you focus your content and ensure that your message is clear.

Defining your purpose in PowerPoint is a critical step in creating a successful presentation. It involves clearly identifying the specific goals and objectives that you want to achieve with your presentation. Here are some tips for defining your purpose in PowerPoint:

- **Identify your audience:** Before you define your purpose, you need to know who your audience is. This will help you tailor your presentation to their needs and interests. Consider factors such as age, education level, and industry to get a better understanding of your audience.

- **Determine your message:** Once you have identified your audience, you need to determine the message you want to convey. Your message should be clear, concise, and relevant to your audience. Make sure it aligns with your overall goals and objectives.

- **Determine your call-to-action:** Your purpose should include a clear call-to-action. What do you want your audience to do after they have seen your presentation? Do you want them to take a specific action, make a decision, or change their behaviour in some way? Make sure your call-to-action is specific, measurable, and achievable.

- **Determine your presentation format:** Depending on your purpose and audience, you may need to choose a specific presentation format. Will you be using a slide show, video, or a combination of both? Make sure your format is appropriate for your message and audience.

- **Determine your presentation length:** Your purpose should also include a clear understanding of how long your presentation should be. This will help you to organize your content and ensure that you don't run out of time.

By defining your purpose in PowerPoint, you can create a presentation that is focused, engaging, and effective. It will help you to achieve your specific goals and objectives, and make sure that your message is received and acted upon by your audience.

Determine your audience:

Understanding your audience is a critical component of planning your presentation. Consider who your audience is and what their needs and interests are. This will help you tailor your message and content to effectively engage them.

Determining your audience in PowerPoint is a crucial step in creating an effective presentation. It involves understanding who your audience is, what their needs and interests are, and tailoring your presentation to meet those needs. Here are some tips for determining your audience in PowerPoint:

- **Research your audience:** Find out as much as you can about your audience, such as their age, gender, education level, job title, and industry. This information will help you understand their needs and interests, and tailor your presentation accordingly.

- **Consider their level of knowledge:** Determine your audience's level of knowledge on the topic you will be presenting. This will help you avoid using jargon or technical terms that may be confusing to them.

- **Consider their motivation:** Why is your audience attending your presentation? Are they there to learn something new, to be entertained, or to solve a problem? Understanding their motivation will help you tailor your presentation to their needs and interests.

- **Consider their culture and background:** If you are presenting to an international audience, it's important to consider their culture and background. Be aware of any cultural norms or taboos that may affect how your audience perceives your message.

- **Consider their learning style:** Some people learn better through visual aids, while others prefer to hear information spoken aloud. Consider incorporating a variety of learning styles into your presentation to appeal to a wider audience.

By understanding your audience in PowerPoint, you can create a presentation that is tailored to their needs and interests. This will help you engage your audience and ensure that your message is received and acted upon.

Develop an outline:

An outline is a useful tool for organizing your content and ensuring that your presentation flows logically. Start with an introduction that captures your audience's attention and clearly states your purpose. Then, develop the main points of your presentation, using headings and subheadings to organize your content. Finally, include a conclusion that summarizes your message and provides a call to action.

Developing an outline in PowerPoint is an important step in organizing your presentation and ensuring that you cover all the key points. Here are some tips for creating an effective outline:

- **Start with a clear introduction:** The introduction should grab the audience's attention, introduce the topic, and preview the main points that will be covered.

- **Organize the body of the presentation:** The body of the presentation should be organized logically, with each point building on the previous one. Use headings and subheadings to break up the presentation into sections, and use bullet points or numbered lists to highlight key information.

- **Include supporting evidence:** It's important to include supporting evidence to back up your claims and make your presentation more persuasive. This could include statistics, examples, or quotes from experts in the field.

- **End with a strong conclusion:** The conclusion should summarize the main points of the presentation and leave the audience with a clear call to action or take-home message.

- **Consider visual aids:** PowerPoint is a visual medium, so it's important to consider how you can use images, charts, and other visual aids to enhance your presentation and reinforce your message.

- **Practice your presentation:** Once you have developed your outline, practice your presentation to ensure that it flows smoothly and that you can deliver it comfortably and confidently.

By developing a clear and well-organized outline in PowerPoint, you can ensure that your presentation is engaging, persuasive, and easy to follow. It will also help you stay focused and on track during the presentation itself.

Choose your visuals:

PowerPoint presentations are often more engaging when they include visuals. Choose visuals that support your message and are relevant to your audience. Use graphs, charts, images, and videos to break up your content and make your presentation more visually appealing.

Visuals are an important part of any PowerPoint presentation. They can help to convey complex information in a more accessible and memorable way, and can also make your presentation more engaging and interesting to your audience. Here are some tips for choosing visuals for your PowerPoint presentation:

- **Choose visuals that support your message:** The visuals you choose should be directly relevant to the points you are making in your presentation. Avoid using visuals just for the sake of adding something extra to your slides.

- **Use high-quality visuals:** Make sure your visuals are clear and easy to see, even from the back of the room.

Use high-resolution images and avoid using low-quality graphics that might appear blurry or pixelated.

- **Keep it simple:** Avoid using visuals that are overly complex or difficult to understand. Instead, opt for simple graphics and images that are easy to interpret and that add to the clarity of your message.

- **Use a consistent visual style:** Use the same colour scheme, font style, and design elements throughout your presentation to create a cohesive look and feel. This will help your audience focus on your message and not get distracted by inconsistent design choices.

- **Use visuals sparingly:** While visuals can be a great addition to your presentation, they can also be distracting if used too frequently. Use visuals sparingly and only when they add value to your message.

- **Avoid copyright infringement:** Make sure that you have permission to use any visuals that are not your own, and always credit your sources appropriately.

By following these tips, you can choose visuals for your PowerPoint presentation that will enhance your message and engage your audience. Remember that the purpose of visuals is to support your message, not to distract from it.

Practice your delivery:

Once you've planned your presentation, it's important to practice your delivery. This will help you refine your message, identify any gaps in your content, and ensure that your presentation is well-timed. Practice speaking clearly and using appropriate body language, and consider recording yourself to evaluate your performance.

Practicing your delivery is an important part of preparing for a PowerPoint presentation. Here are some tips to help you practice effectively:

- **Time yourself:** Time your presentation to ensure that it fits within the allotted time. This will help you pace yourself during the actual presentation and avoid rushing through your slides.

- **Practice with your visuals:** Use your slides when practicing your presentation to ensure that your delivery matches your visuals. This will help you identify any areas where your message might be unclear or where you need to adjust your delivery to better support your message.

- **Record yourself:** Use a smartphone or camera to record yourself practicing your presentation. This will allow you to review your delivery and identify areas where you can improve.

- **Practice in front of others:** Practice in front of friends or colleagues to get feedback on your delivery. Ask for honest feedback on areas where you can improve, and use this feedback to adjust your delivery before your actual presentation.

- **Rehearse your opening and closing:** Practice your opening and closing statements to ensure that they are engaging and effective. This will help you capture your audience's attention at the beginning of your presentation and leave a lasting impression at the end.

By practicing your delivery, you can feel more confident and prepared when it comes time to deliver your PowerPoint presentation. Remember to focus on your message, pace yourself, and engage your audience to deliver an effective and memorable presentation.

Edit and refine:

After you've practiced your presentation, take some time to review and edit your content. Look for areas where you can clarify your message or tighten up your content. Consider getting feedback from others to identify any areas for improvement.

Editing and refining your PowerPoint presentation is a crucial step in the preparation process. Here are some tips to help you edit and refine your presentation:

- **Review for clarity and organization:** Go through your presentation to ensure that it is clear, organized, and easy to follow. This will help your audience understand your message and stay engaged throughout your presentation.

- **Check for consistency:** Ensure that your presentation is consistent in terms of formatting, font sizes, and colours. This will give your presentation a professional and polished look.

- **Simplify your message:** Remove any unnecessary information and simplify your message. This will help your audience understand and remember your key points.

- **Rehearse with your revised presentation**: Practice your presentation with your revised slides to ensure that your delivery matches your new message.

- **Get feedback:** Show your revised presentation to colleagues, friends, or family members and ask for feedback. This will help you identify any areas that still need improvement and give you valuable insights on how to refine your presentation further.

By editing and refining your PowerPoint presentation, you can ensure that your message is clear, concise, and engaging for your audience. Remember to review for clarity and organization, simplify your message, and get feedback to ensure that your final presentation is effective and memorable.

Overall, planning your presentation is a critical step in creating an effective PowerPoint presentation. By defining your purpose, identifying your audience, developing an outline, choosing visuals, practicing your delivery, and editing and refining your content, you can create a presentation that effectively communicates your message and engages your audience.

4

Designing Your Presentation

The design of your PowerPoint presentation is just as important as the content. Your slides should be visually appealing and easy to read, with graphics and images that enhance your message.

In this chapter, we will explore the different design elements of a PowerPoint presentation, including how to choose the right font and colour scheme, how to use images and graphics, and how to create effective charts and diagrams.

Designing your PowerPoint presentation is a crucial step in creating an effective and engaging presentation. Here are some tips for designing your presentation in PowerPoint:

Choose a consistent design:

Your presentation should have a consistent design throughout. Choose a theme that reflects your brand or message and use it consistently on each slide. This will help create a cohesive and professional-looking presentation.

Choosing a consistent design in PowerPoint is essential for creating a professional and visually appealing presentation. Here are some tips to help you choose a consistent design:

- **Choose a theme:** A theme in PowerPoint is a pre-set collection of design elements, such as fonts, colours, and background styles. Choose a theme that suits your presentation and stick to it throughout your presentation.

- **Use a consistent colour scheme:** Select a colour scheme that matches your theme and stick to it. Use the same colours throughout your presentation for titles, subtitles, bullet points, and images.

- **Select fonts carefully:** Choose two or three fonts that complement each other and use them consistently throughout your presentation. Use one font for headings and another for body text.

- **Use consistent slide layouts:** Use the same slide layout throughout your presentation for consistency. This helps your audience focus on your message rather than being distracted by design changes.

- **Add visual elements:** Use images, charts, and graphs to enhance your presentation. Make sure they are consistent in style and quality.

- **Avoid using too many animations**: Animations can be distracting and take away from your message. Use them sparingly and consistently throughout your presentation.

By choosing a consistent design, you can create a professional and visually appealing presentation that helps your audience focus on your message. Remember to choose a theme, use a consistent colour scheme and fonts, use consistent slide layouts, and avoid using too many animations.

Use legible fonts:

Make sure the fonts you use are easy to read. Avoid using decorative or ornate fonts, and stick to simple, legible fonts like

Arial or Calibri. Use a font size that is large enough to be read from a distance.

Using legible fonts in PowerPoint is crucial for ensuring that your audience can read your presentation content easily. Here are some tips for choosing and using legible fonts:

- **Use sans-serif fonts:** Sans-serif fonts like Arial and Calibri are easier to read on screens than serif fonts like Times New Roman.

- **Avoid decorative fonts:** Decorative fonts may look nice, but they can be hard to read, especially from a distance.

- **Use a large font size:** Use a font size that is large enough to be read from the back of the room. A font size of at least 24 points is recommended.

- **Use a consistent font:** Use the same font throughout your presentation. This will help your audience focus on your message rather than being distracted by different fonts.

- **Use contrasting colours:** Use a dark font colour on a light background, or a light font colour on a dark background. This will ensure that your text is easy to read.

- **Use bullet points:** Use bullet points to break up your text and make it easier to read. Make sure your bullet points are consistent in size and style.

By using legible fonts in PowerPoint, you can make sure that your audience can easily read and understand your presentation content. Remember to use sans-serif fonts, avoid decorative fonts, use a large font size, use a consistent font, use contrasting colours, and use bullet points.

Use contrasting colours:

Use contrasting colours for text and background to ensure that your content is legible. Avoid using colours that clash or are difficult to read, and use colours that reflect your brand or message.
Using contrasting colours in PowerPoint is important for ensuring that your text and visual elements are easily readable and stand out on the slide. Here are some tips for using contrasting colours effectively:

- **Use high contrast colours:** High contrast colours, such as black and white, or dark blue and light yellow, will make your text and visual elements stand out and be easily readable.

- **Avoid low contrast colours:** Low contrast colours, such as light grey on a white background, can be hard to read, especially for people with visual impairments.

- **Use complementary colours:** Complementary colours, such as blue and orange or green and purple, can create a visually appealing contrast that draws attention to your content.

- **Be consistent:** Use a consistent colour scheme throughout your presentation to make it easier for your audience to follow along.

- **Use colour to emphasize key points:** Use colour to draw attention to important points or to highlight specific text or visual elements on the slide.

- **Test your colours on different devices**: Make sure to test your colours on different devices to ensure that they are readable and effective on a variety of screens.

By using contrasting colours in PowerPoint, you can create slides that are visually engaging and easy to read for your audience. Remember to use high contrast colours, avoid low contrast colours, use complementary colours, be consistent, use colour to emphasize key points, and test your colours on different devices.

Keep it simple:

Avoid cluttering your slides with too much text or too many images. Use white space to make your content easier to read, and focus on one idea per slide. This will help your audience better understand your message and stay engaged with your presentation.

Keeping your PowerPoint presentations simple can help to ensure that your audience is able to focus on your message and not get distracted by unnecessary elements. Here are some tips for keeping your presentations simple:

- **Limit the number of slides:** Instead of overwhelming your audience with a large number of slides, focus on creating a few key slides that effectively communicate your message.

- **Use clear and concise language:** Avoid using complex language or jargon that your audience may not understand. Instead, use clear and concise language that is easy to understand.

- **Use bullet points:** Bullet points can help to break up your content into digestible pieces and make it easier for your audience to follow along.

- **Use simple graphics:** Avoid using overly complex graphics or charts that may be difficult to interpret. Instead, use simple graphics and charts that are easy to understand.

- **Avoid clutter:** Don't clutter your slides with too much text, graphics, or other elements. Keep it simple and focused on your message.

- **Use white space:** White space can help to make your slides look clean and uncluttered. Use it to your advantage by leaving plenty of space around your text and graphics.

- **Use minimal text:** Avoid cramming too much text onto a slide. Instead, use bullet points and short phrases to convey your message.

- **Limit the number of slides:** A good rule of thumb is to limit your presentation to one slide per minute of speaking time. This helps to keep your presentation focused and on track.

- **Avoid flashy animations and transitions:** While PowerPoint offers a range of animations and transitions, it's best to keep them simple and subtle. Avoid using flashy animations and transitions that may distract from your message.

By keeping your PowerPoint presentations simple, you can ensure that your message is clear and easy to understand for your audience. Use minimal text, clear and concise language, limit the number of slides, use simple graphics, use white space, and avoid flashy animations and transitions.

Use visuals:

Visuals can be an effective tool for engaging your audience and making your presentation more memorable. Use high-quality images, charts, graphs, and videos to help illustrate your points and break up your content.

Visuals are an essential component of any PowerPoint presentation. They help to break up the monotony of text and keep the audience engaged. When used effectively, visuals can reinforce your message, clarify complex concepts, and create an emotional connection with your audience. Here are some tips for using visuals in your PowerPoint presentation:

- **Choose relevant visuals:** The visuals you use should be directly related to the content of your presentation. Avoid using irrelevant or distracting visuals that can confuse or mislead your audience.

- **Use high-quality visuals:** Low-quality visuals can be distracting and unprofessional. Make sure the images you use are high-quality and appropriate for the size of the screen.

- **Keep it simple:** Just like your text, your visuals should be simple and easy to understand. Avoid cluttered or busy visuals that can overwhelm your audience.

- **Use appropriate charts and graphs:** If you're presenting data or statistics, use appropriate charts and graphs to make it easier for your audience to understand the information.

- **Use animation and transitions sparingly:** Animation and transitions can add visual interest to your presentation, but use them sparingly. Too much animation can be distracting and take away from your message.

- **Use colour effectively:** Colour can be a powerful tool in your presentation. Use colours that are consistent with your brand or theme, and use contrasting colours to draw attention to important information.

- **Use relevant videos:** If you have a relevant video, you can incorporate it into your presentation to make it more engaging. Just make sure it's high-quality and appropriate for your audience.

In summary, using visuals can greatly enhance the impact of your PowerPoint presentation. Just be sure to choose high-quality and relevant visuals, keep it simple, and use colours and animations effectively.

Be consistent with animations:

Animations can add interest to your presentation, but use them sparingly and consistently. Use the same animation throughout your presentation to create a sense of continuity.

Animations in PowerPoint can be a powerful tool to enhance the visual appeal of your presentation and make it more engaging. However, it is important to use animations in a consistent manner to avoid overwhelming or confusing your audience.

Here are some tips for using animations effectively in your PowerPoint presentation:

- **Choose a consistent animation scheme:** Pick one or two animation schemes that you will use consistently throughout your presentation. This will help create a cohesive visual experience for your audience.

- **Use animations to enhance your message:** Use animations sparingly to emphasize key points or to help illustrate complex ideas. Avoid using animations for the sake of using them, as this can become distracting and take away from the overall message of your presentation.

- **Keep it simple:** Avoid using too many animations or complex animations that may be difficult for your audience to follow. Stick to simple and straightforward animations that can be easily understood.

- **Use animations to build anticipation:** Consider using animations to build anticipation or reveal information in a creative way. For example, you can use a simple fade-in animation to reveal a new bullet point or image.

- **Practice your timing:** Make sure to practice the timing of your animations to ensure they are synced with your delivery. This will help prevent awkward pauses or rushed transitions.

Overall, animations can be a great addition to your PowerPoint presentation if used effectively and in a consistent manner. By following these tips, you can create a more engaging and memorable presentation for your audience.

Test your presentation:

Before delivering your presentation, test it to make sure that all of the visuals, animations, and transitions work properly. Make sure that all of the text is legible and that the images and videos are high-quality.

Testing your presentation in PowerPoint is an essential step in ensuring a smooth and effective delivery. By testing your presentation beforehand, you can identify and address any issues or glitches that might arise during your actual presentation. Here are some tips for testing your presentation in PowerPoint:

- **Test on the actual presentation computer:** It is crucial to test your presentation on the actual computer you will be using during your presentation. This will help you avoid any issues with compatibility or missing fonts, images, or videos.

- **Check for broken links**: If you have any links or external sources in your presentation, make sure they are all working correctly. Broken links can cause disruptions in your presentation and leave a negative impression on your audience.

- **Review animations and transitions:** Make sure all animations and transitions are working correctly and are consistent throughout the presentation. It's also essential to ensure that they are not too distracting or overdone.

- **Practice your delivery:** Practice your presentation as if you were in front of your audience. This will help you identify any issues with timing, flow, or organization and allow you to make any necessary adjustments.

- **Rehearse with a colleague:** Consider rehearsing your presentation with a colleague or friend who can provide you with feedback on your delivery and overall effectiveness of the presentation.

By following these tips, you can ensure that your presentation is smooth, error-free, and engaging for your audience.

Overall, designing your PowerPoint presentation is a crucial step in creating an effective and engaging presentation. By choosing a consistent design, using legible fonts, using contrasting colours, keeping it simple, using visuals, being consistent with animations, and testing your presentation, you can create a presentation that effectively communicates your message and engages your audience.

5

Adding Interactivity and Engagement

To keep your audience engaged, your PowerPoint presentation should be interactive and include opportunities for participation. This can include polls, quizzes, and discussion questions.

In this chapter, we will explore how to add interactivity to your PowerPoint presentation, including how to use animations and transitions, how to create interactive slides, and how to engage your audience throughout your presentation.

Adding interactivity and engagement to your PowerPoint presentation can help keep your audience engaged and increase their understanding of your message. Here are some ways to add interactivity and engagement to your PowerPoint presentation:

Polls and surveys:

Use polls and surveys to engage your audience and gather feedback on your message. You can use a third-party tool to create the poll or survey and embed it into your presentation.

Polls and surveys are great interactive features that can be used in PowerPoint presentations to engage the audience and gather feedback. Polls are used to gather the audience's opinion on a specific topic, while surveys are used to gather more detailed information about the audience's background or preferences.

To create polls and surveys in PowerPoint, you can use third-party tools such as Mentimeter, Poll Everywhere, or Kahoot.

These tools allow you to create interactive questions and display the results in real-time on your presentation.

When creating a poll or survey, it's important to keep the questions clear and concise. Avoid using technical jargon or complex language that could confuse the audience. Also, consider the amount of time you have for the presentation and how many questions you can realistically ask.

It's also important to choose the right type of question for your poll or survey. Open-ended questions allow the audience to provide more detailed responses, while closed-ended questions are quicker and easier to answer. You can also use multiple-choice questions, rating scales, or ranking questions to gather specific types of feedback.

During the presentation, make sure to explain the purpose of the poll or survey and how the results will be used. Encourage the audience to participate by explaining the benefits of their feedback and keeping the questions interesting and engaging.

Finally, make sure to analyse the results after the presentation and use them to improve future presentations or to make informed decisions.

Quizzes and games:

Use quizzes or games to test your audience's knowledge and keep them engaged. You can use a third-party tool to create the quiz or game and embed it into your presentation.

One effective way to add interactivity and engagement to your PowerPoint presentation is by incorporating quizzes and games. This can be especially useful in educational or training presentations, where you want to test your audience's understanding of the material.

Here are some tips for incorporating quizzes and games into your PowerPoint presentation:

- **Decide on the type of quiz or game:** There are many types of quizzes and games you can create in PowerPoint, including multiple-choice questions, true/false questions, matching games, and even interactive board games. Choose the type that best suits your audience and the content of your presentation.

- **Use templates:** If you're new to creating quizzes and games in PowerPoint, consider using pre-made templates. Many templates are available online that you can customize to fit your needs.

- **Keep it relevant:** Make sure that the questions and games you include are relevant to the content of your presentation. They should be designed to reinforce the key concepts and ideas you are trying to convey.

- **Make it visually appealing:** Use images and animations to make your quizzes and games visually engaging. This will help keep your audience's attention and make the experience more enjoyable.

- **Provide feedback:** Whether it's immediate feedback after each question or a summary at the end of the quiz or game, provide feedback to your audience. This will help reinforce the concepts and ideas you are trying to teach.

- **Keep it balanced:** While quizzes and games can be a great way to engage your audience, don't overdo it. Make sure that the quizzes and games you include don't take away from the overall message of your presentation.

By incorporating quizzes and games into your PowerPoint presentation, you can add an element of fun and interactivity that will keep your audience engaged and help reinforce the key concepts and ideas you are trying to convey.

Interactive graphics:

Use interactive graphics, such as timelines, maps, or flowcharts, to help illustrate your message and engage your audience. You can use built-in PowerPoint tools or third-party tools to create these graphics.

Interactive graphics can be a great way to engage your audience and convey complex information in a clear and memorable way. In PowerPoint, there are a variety of tools you can use to create interactive graphics, such as:

- **SmartArt:** SmartArt is a built-in tool that allows you to create professional-looking diagrams, charts, and other graphics quickly and easily. You can choose from a variety of SmartArt graphics, including process diagrams, cycle diagrams, hierarchy diagrams, and more.

- **Hyperlinks:** Hyperlinks allow you to create clickable elements within your presentation that take your audience to another slide or even another document or website. This can be useful for creating interactive maps, timelines, or diagrams that allow your audience to explore different elements of the graphic.

- **Action Buttons:** Action buttons are pre-designed buttons that you can add to your slides to create interactivity. You can choose from a variety of shapes and styles, and each button can be programmed to perform a different action, such as taking the viewer to a specific slide or playing a video.

- **Animations:** Animations can be used to create interactive graphics that move or change based on viewer interactions. For example, you can use animations to create a flipbook-style animation that lets the viewer interact with different elements of the graphic.

- **3D Models:** PowerPoint also has built-in support for 3D models, which can be used to create interactive diagrams, models, and other graphics. You can import 3D models from external sources or create your own using PowerPoint's built-in tools.

When creating interactive graphics in PowerPoint, it's important to keep in mind the needs and interests of your audience. Make sure that the interactive elements are relevant to the topic at hand and are designed in a way that is easy for viewers to understand and engage with.

Video and audio:

Incorporate video or audio into your presentation to add interest and engagement. You can use built-in PowerPoint tools to add video or audio, or embed a third-party video or audio player.

Using videos and audios in PowerPoint presentations can help to make the presentation more engaging and dynamic. It can also be useful for demonstrating a process or product that would be difficult to explain with just words or images. Here are some tips on using video and audio in PowerPoint:

- **Choose high-quality media:** When selecting a video or audio file to include in your presentation, make sure that it is high quality and clear. Poor quality media can detract from the overall professionalism of your presentation.

- **Keep it short:** Videos and audio clips should be brief, ideally no longer than a few minutes. Longer videos or audio clips may cause your audience to lose interest or become distracted.

- **Embed media files:** Rather than linking to external media files, it is recommended to embed videos and audio files into your PowerPoint presentation. This ensures that the media will play properly and eliminates the need for an internet connection during your presentation.

- **Check for compatibility:** Make sure that your video or audio file is compatible with PowerPoint and the computer you will be using for your presentation. Test your presentation on the computer you will be using ahead of time to ensure that your media files play correctly.

- **Use media strategically:** Consider using video and audio strategically to enhance your presentation, such as demonstrating a process or highlighting a key point. Don't overuse videos or audio, as it can become distracting or overwhelming for your audience.

- **Provide captions:** If your video includes dialogue, it is a good idea to provide captions or a transcript to ensure that all audience members can follow along. This is especially important for those with hearing impairments.

Overall, videos and audio can be a powerful tool for enhancing your PowerPoint presentation, but it is important to use them strategically and thoughtfully.

Hyperlinks:

Use hyperlinks to guide your audience through your presentation and provide additional information or resources. You can link to external websites, documents, or other resources.

Hyperlinks are an effective way to add interactivity to your PowerPoint presentation. Hyperlinks allow you to link to other slides within your presentation, external websites, documents, and even email addresses.

To add a hyperlink, first, select the text or object you want to use as a hyperlink. Then, click on the Insert tab on the ribbon and select Hyperlink. In the Insert Hyperlink dialog box, you can choose to link to an existing file or web page, create a new email message, or link to a specific slide within your presentation.

When linking to another slide within your presentation, select "Place in This Document" in the Link to section and choose the slide you want to link to from the list of available slides.

To test your hyperlink, enter Slide Show mode and click on the linked text or object. If the hyperlink is to an external website or document, make sure that you have an internet connection and the appropriate software installed to view the file.

Hyperlinks can also be used to navigate within your presentation. For example, you can add hyperlinks to your table of contents slide that link to the relevant sections of your presentation. This allows your audience to easily jump to the information they are interested in.

When using hyperlinks, it's important to make sure they are visible and easily identifiable to your audience. Use underlining, bolding, or a different colour to make the hyperlink stand out from the surrounding text.

Overall, hyperlinks are a useful tool for creating interactive and engaging PowerPoint presentations. By adding hyperlinks, you can make your presentation more informative, user-friendly, and dynamic.

Interactive activities:

Use interactive activities, such as brainstorming sessions or small group discussions, to engage your audience and encourage participation.

Interactive activities in PowerPoint can be a great way to engage your audience and make your presentation more memorable. Here are some examples of interactive activities that you can incorporate into your PowerPoint presentation:

- **Drag and drop activities:** You can create interactive activities that require your audience to drag and drop elements on the screen. This can be particularly useful for activities that involve sorting or matching.

- **Hotspot activities:** Hotspot activities involve placing clickable areas on a slide that take the user to another slide or perform an action when clicked. This can be used to create interactive maps, diagrams or menus.

- **Interactive timelines**: You can create interactive timelines that allow users to explore different events or periods in more detail. This can be particularly useful for historical or scientific presentations.

- **Interactive quizzes:** You can create interactive quizzes that test your audience's knowledge on a particular subject. You can use multiple-choice questions, true/false questions, or fill-in-the-blank questions.

- **Live polls:** You can use live polls to gather feedback from your audience in real-time. This can be a great way to gauge the level of understanding of your topic or get opinions on a particular issue.

- **Virtual reality:** You can use virtual reality to create immersive experiences for your audience. This can be particularly useful for educational or training presentations.

When creating interactive activities in PowerPoint, it's important to keep in mind the purpose and audience of your presentation. The activities should be relevant to the content and should enhance the overall message you are trying to convey. Additionally, make sure the interactive elements are easy to use and understand, and avoid making the activities too complex or time-consuming.

Live polling:

Use live polling tools to allow your audience to vote on topics or provide feedback in real-time. You can use third-party tools or built-in PowerPoint tools to create live polls.

Live polling is an interactive feature in PowerPoint that allows presenters to ask real-time questions to their audience and receive immediate feedback. It is a great way to engage the audience and make presentations more dynamic and interactive.

To use live polling in PowerPoint, you need to have an active internet connection and a third-party polling tool. Some popular polling tools that integrate with PowerPoint include Poll Everywhere, Mentimeter, and Slido.

Once you have chosen a polling tool, you can create your questions and add them to your PowerPoint presentation. During the presentation, you can display the questions on your slides and ask your audience to respond using their smartphones or other devices. The responses are then collected in real-time and displayed on the slide.

Live polling can be used in a variety of settings, from classroom lectures and corporate training sessions to conferences and public speaking events. It can be used to gather feedback, test knowledge, or stimulate discussion.

When using live polling in PowerPoint, it is important to keep in mind the following tips:

a) Keep the questions short and clear
b) Avoid using complex or technical language
c) Test the polling system before the presentation
d) Provide clear instructions to the audience on how to participate
e) Consider using multiple-choice or true/false questions for easier data analysis.

Overall, live polling is a powerful tool that can help to make presentations more engaging and interactive, and can help to increase audience participation and feedback.

Overall, adding interactivity and engagement to your PowerPoint presentation can help keep your audience engaged and increase their understanding of your message. By using polls and surveys, quizzes and games, interactive graphics, video and audio, hyperlinks, interactive activities, and live polling, you can create a dynamic and engaging presentation.

6

Practicing Your Presentation

Once you have created your PowerPoint presentation, you need to practice delivering it. This will help you become familiar with your content, and ensure that you are confident and prepared when it is time to present.

In this segment, we will explore how to practice your presentation effectively, including how to rehearse your delivery, how to handle nerves and anxiety, and how to use feedback to improve your presentation.

Practicing your PowerPoint presentation is an essential step in ensuring that it runs smoothly and that you deliver a confident and engaging presentation. Here are some tips for practicing your presentation in PowerPoint:

Rehearse your presentation:

Rehearse your presentation several times to familiarize yourself with the content and timing. This will help you feel more confident and comfortable during the actual presentation.

Rehearsing your presentation in PowerPoint is an important step to ensure that you are confident and prepared when delivering your presentation to your audience. By rehearsing, you can identify areas where you may stumble or forget important information, and you can work out the timing of your presentation. Here are some tips on how to rehearse your presentation effectively:

- **Practice with the actual equipment:** Rehearse your presentation using the same computer, projector, and microphone that you will be using during the actual presentation. This will help you become familiar with the equipment and avoid any technical difficulties during the actual presentation.

- **Practice in the same environment:** Try to rehearse your presentation in the same environment where you will be delivering it. This will help you get used to the space and any potential distractions or technical issues.

- **Practice out loud:** Don't just read your slides silently. Practice speaking out loud, as this will help you get used to the sound of your own voice and the rhythm of your presentation.

- **Practice your delivery:** Pay attention to your body language, tone of voice, and pacing. Try to speak clearly and confidently and use appropriate gestures and facial expressions to engage your audience.

- **Rehearse in front of others:** Practice your presentation in front of friends or colleagues and ask for their feedback. This will help you identify any areas that need improvement and make necessary adjustments before the actual presentation.

- **Time yourself:** Make sure to time yourself when rehearsing your presentation to ensure that you stay within the allotted time. This will help you pace your presentation and avoid rushing or speaking too slowly. Use a timer or stopwatch to time yourself as you rehearse. This will give you a good idea of how long your presentation will take and help you adjust the timing if needed.

- **Record and review:** Record yourself rehearsing your presentation and review the footage to identify any areas that need improvement. Use a recording device, such as a video camera or smartphone, to record yourself rehearsing. This will allow you to watch and critique your performance, and identify areas for improvement. This can be especially helpful for identifying issues with pacing, delivery, or visual aids.

- **Repeat:** Repeat the rehearsal process multiple times until you feel confident and prepared to deliver your presentation to your audience. The more you rehearse, the more comfortable and confident you will become with your material.

- **Rehearse with a friend or colleague**: It can be helpful to rehearse your presentation with a friend or colleague who can provide feedback and constructive criticism.

- **Make adjustments:** As you rehearse, take note of any areas where you stumble or forget information, and make adjustments to your slides or notes to help you remember.

- **Use a timer:** Use a timer to track your time and ensure that you stay within the allotted time for your presentation. This will help you pace yourself and avoid rushing through the content or running out of time.

- **Practice transitions:** Practice your slide transitions and animations to make sure they run smoothly and don't distract from your message.

- **Practice speaking:** Practice speaking clearly and confidently, and avoid using filler words like "um" or "ah." Speak at a steady pace and use pauses to emphasize key points.

- **Get feedback:** Practice your presentation in front of friends, family, or colleagues and ask for their feedback. This can help you identify areas where you can improve and make your presentation more effective.

Overall, practicing your PowerPoint presentation is a crucial step in ensuring that you deliver a confident and engaging presentation. By rehearsing your presentation, using a timer, practicing transitions, speaking clearly, getting feedback, recording yourself, and rehearsing with the equipment, you can feel more confident and prepared for your presentation.

7

Delivering Your Presentation

When it comes time to deliver your PowerPoint presentation, you want to be confident, engaging, and prepared. This means being familiar with your content, speaking clearly and confidently, and engaging with your audience.

In this chapter, we will explore how to deliver your PowerPoint presentation effectively, including how to engage your audience, how to handle questions and feedback, and how to make a lasting impression.

Delivering your PowerPoint presentation is the most crucial part of the process. Here are some tips for delivering an effective and engaging presentation:

Start with an attention-grabbing opening:

Begin your presentation with a strong and attention-grabbing opening to hook your audience's attention. This can be a powerful statistic, an engaging story, or a provocative question.

Starting a presentation with an attention-grabbing opening is crucial to engaging your audience and setting the tone for the rest of your presentation. There are many ways to open a presentation, such as telling a story, asking a thought-provoking question, sharing a surprising fact, or using a relevant quote.

The key is to think about your audience and what will capture their interest and attention. You want to make sure that your opening is relevant to your presentation topic and sets the stage for what you'll be discussing.

An attention-grabbing opening can help you establish credibility, build rapport with your audience, and create a sense of excitement and anticipation for the rest of your presentation. It can also help you overcome any initial resistance or scepticism your audience may have towards your topic.

To make your opening even more effective, consider using visual aids or multimedia elements such as images, videos, or animations. This can help bring your opening to life and capture your audience's attention even more effectively.

Speak clearly and confidently:

Speak clearly and confidently to convey your message effectively. Avoid speaking too quickly or softly, and use pauses and inflections to emphasize key points.

Speaking clearly and confidently is essential for delivering an effective presentation in PowerPoint. Here are some tips to help you speak clearly and confidently:

- **Speak slowly:** Speaking too quickly can make it difficult for your audience to understand you. Make a conscious effort to speak slowly and enunciate your words clearly.

- **Use a conversational tone**: Use a conversational tone when presenting, as if you were having a one-on-one conversation with someone. This will help you connect with your audience and make them feel more comfortable.

- **Use body language:** Body language is an important aspect of public speaking. Use your hands and body to emphasize key points and help your audience stay engaged.

- **Maintain eye contact:** Make eye contact with your audience throughout your presentation. This will help you connect with your audience and keep their attention.

- **Use pauses:** Pausing is an effective way to emphasize key points and give your audience time to absorb what you are saying.

- **Project your voice:** Make sure that you project your voice so that everyone in the room can hear you clearly. This is especially important if you are presenting in a large room or auditorium.

By following these tips, you can speak clearly and confidently, and deliver a successful presentation in PowerPoint.

Maintain eye contact:

Maintain eye contact with your audience to establish a connection and keep them engaged. Scan the room and make eye contact with different members of the audience.

Maintaining eye contact is an important aspect of delivering an effective presentation in PowerPoint. Eye contact helps establish a connection with the audience and keeps them engaged. Here are some tips on maintaining eye contact during your presentation:

- **Look at your audience:** Make a conscious effort to look at your audience while speaking. Scan the room and make eye contact with individuals in different parts of the audience.

- **Use visual aids:** Visual aids like images, graphs, and videos can help you maintain eye contact with your audience. Instead of reading from your slides, use visual aids as cues to help you remember the main points you want to make.

- **Avoid distractions:** Distractions such as your notes, your phone, or other objects can take your attention away from your audience. Make sure to keep all distractions out of sight to help you stay focused on your audience.

- **Pause:** Pausing at key points in your presentation can help you maintain eye contact with your audience. Take a moment to look at your audience and allow them time to process the information you've presented.

- **Practice:** Practicing your presentation can help you feel more confident and comfortable, which in turn can help you maintain eye contact with your audience. Practice in front of a mirror or with a friend to get feedback on your eye contact and body language.

Use body language:

Use body language to convey confidence and enthusiasm. Stand up straight, use gestures to emphasize key points, and move around the stage to keep the audience engaged.

Using appropriate body language during a presentation can help you convey your message more effectively and connect with your audience. Here are some tips for using body language in your PowerPoint presentation:

- **Stand up straight:** Good posture communicates confidence and authority. Stand up straight and avoid slouching or leaning on the podium.

- **Make eye contact:** Maintain eye contact with your audience to engage them and convey your confidence. Look around the room and make eye contact with different individuals, not just one person or the same few people throughout the presentation.

- **Use hand gestures:** Appropriate hand gestures can help emphasize your points and convey enthusiasm. However, be careful not to overuse or distract with excessive hand movements.

- **Move around:** Moving around the stage or platform can help you engage with different areas of the audience and keep their attention. However, avoid pacing or walking too much, which can be distracting.

- **Use facial expressions:** Your facial expressions can convey your emotions and help you connect with your audience. Use appropriate expressions to match the tone and content of your presentation.

Remember, body language can also vary depending on the context and the audience you are presenting to. Practice and adjust your body language to best match your presentation style and audience.

Stay on topic:

Stay on topic and avoid going off on tangents. Stick to your main points and use supporting evidence to reinforce your message.

Staying on topic is an important aspect of delivering an effective presentation in PowerPoint. It involves focusing on the main points of your presentation and avoiding going off on tangents that are not relevant to the topic.

Here are some tips on how to stay on topic during your presentation:

- **Have a clear outline:** Before you start your presentation, create a clear outline of your main points. This will help you stay focused and avoid going off on tangents.

- **Practice:** Rehearse your presentation multiple times to ensure that you are comfortable with the material and can deliver it smoothly.

- **Use visual aids:** Visual aids such as PowerPoint slides can help you stay on topic by providing a structure for your presentation.

- **Keep it concise:** Try to keep your presentation concise and avoid including unnecessary information that may distract from the main topic.

- **Pause and regroup:** If you find yourself straying from the topic, take a pause, and regroup. Take a deep breath, look at your notes, and refocus on the main points of your presentation.

Overall, staying on topic is essential for delivering a clear and effective presentation that will engage your audience and leave a lasting impression.

Use visual aids effectively:

Use your visual aids, such as PowerPoint slides or handouts, effectively to reinforce your message. Avoid reading from your slides or handouts, and use them to supplement your presentation.

Using visual aids effectively is an important aspect of delivering a successful presentation in PowerPoint. Here are some tips to help you use visual aids effectively:

- **Keep it simple:** The purpose of visual aids is to enhance your presentation, not detract from it. Keep your slides simple and uncluttered, with minimal text and clear, high-quality images.

- **Use relevant visuals:** Use visuals that are relevant to the topic you are presenting. This will help your audience better understand and retain the information you are presenting.

- **Use large fonts:** Make sure the fonts you use on your slides are large enough to be easily read from the back of the room.

- **Use contrasting colours:** Use contrasting colours for your text and background to make your slides easy to read.

- **Use animations and transitions sparingly:** While animations and transitions can be fun and engaging, too many can be distracting and take away from your presentation.

- **Use multimedia:** Incorporate multimedia elements such as videos, images, and audio to add interest and variety to your presentation.

- **Practice using your visual aids:** Make sure you practice using your visual aids before the presentation to ensure they work properly and that you are comfortable using them.

Remember, visual aids should enhance your presentation, not be the main focus. Use them strategically and sparingly to help your audience better understand and remember the information you are presenting.

Engage your audience:

Engage your audience by asking questions, encouraging discussion, or using interactive activities. This can help keep them engaged and reinforce your message.

Engaging your audience is crucial to delivering a successful presentation in PowerPoint. Here are some tips for how to do so:

- **Use storytelling:** People tend to remember stories better than facts and figures, so try to incorporate some storytelling into your presentation. This can be a personal anecdote, a case study, or a hypothetical scenario.

- **Ask questions:** Asking questions throughout your presentation can help keep your audience engaged and actively thinking about the topic. Make sure to pause and give your audience time to answer before moving on.

- **Use humour:** Humour can be a powerful tool for engaging your audience and making your presentation more memorable. Just make sure to keep it appropriate and relevant to your topic.

- **Encourage participation**: You can also engage your audience by encouraging them to participate in the presentation. This can be through activities like polls, quizzes, or group discussions.

- **Use visual aids:** Visual aids like charts, graphs, and images can help illustrate your points and keep your audience engaged. Just make sure not to overload your slides with too much information.

- **Speak to your audience's needs:** Make sure your presentation is tailored to your audience's needs and interests. Use examples and case studies that are relevant to their industry or field.

- **Use body language:** Using appropriate body language, such as hand gestures and facial expressions, can help you connect with your audience and emphasize key points in your presentation.

Overall, engaging your audience requires a mix of thoughtful planning, engaging visuals, and effective communication techniques. By incorporating these strategies into your PowerPoint presentation, you can deliver a presentation that captures your audience's attention and keeps them engaged throughout.

End with a strong conclusion:

End your presentation with a strong and memorable conclusion that summarizes your message and leaves a lasting impression on your audience.

Ending a presentation with a strong conclusion is just as important as starting it with an attention-grabbing opening. A strong conclusion will help reinforce the key points of your presentation and leave a lasting impression on your audience. Here are some tips for ending your presentation on a high note:

- **Summarize your main points:** Review the main points you covered in your presentation, making sure to emphasize their importance.

- **Restate your purpose:** Remind your audience of your presentation's purpose and how you have achieved it.

- **Call to action:** Encourage your audience to take action or consider next steps. This could be anything from asking for feedback to inviting them to sign up for a service or product.

- **Use a memorable quote:** End with a memorable quote that reinforces your message or sums up your presentation.

- **Provide additional resources:** Offer your audience additional resources for further reading or research related to your topic.

- **End on a positive note:** End your presentation on a positive and upbeat note to leave your audience feeling energized and motivated.

Remember, the conclusion of your presentation is your last chance to make a lasting impression on your audience, so make it count!

Overall, delivering an effective PowerPoint presentation requires clear and confident speaking, engaging body language, effective use of visual aids, and audience engagement. By following these tips, you can deliver an effective and engaging presentation that leaves a lasting impression on your audience.

8

Understanding the Slides

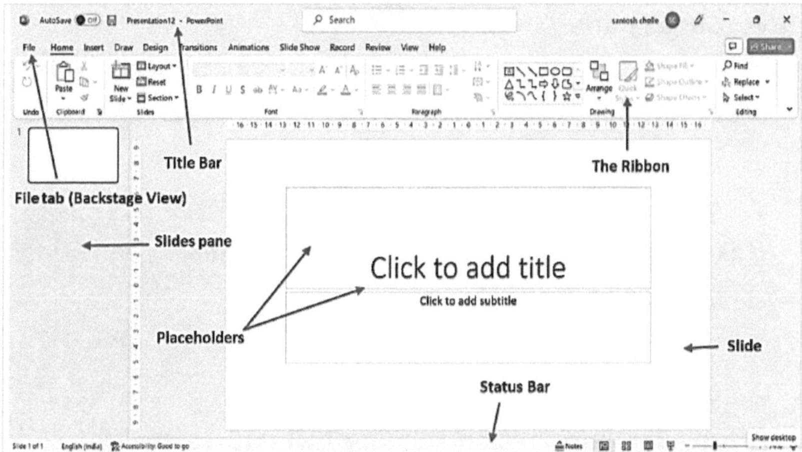

- **Title Bar**

Shows the name of the application and the file currently in use.

- **The Ribbon**

Shows numerous functions and tools available to work with your presentation.

- **Quick Access Toolbar**

Enables you to customise the toolbar to contain the commands you use most frequently.

- **File tab (Backstage View)**

Provides access to basic commands such as New, Open, Save, Print and Share plus access to customise the application.

- **Slides pane**

Shows a thumbnail version of each slide within presentation.

- **Slide**

This area which will be displayed as full screen when viewed in Slide Show mode.

- **Status Bar**

It provides information relating to features such as slide number, spell check and shortcuts to Notes, Comments, various different views and zoom functions.

- **Placeholders**

Where you can add text, and insert elements such as images or tables.

Placeholder in PowerPoint

Have you ever wondered about using a placeholder in PowerPoint? Placeholders are identified by the dotted external border surrounding the containers on a slide. They are specifically used to position different types of content on a slide, and they are preformatted to provide consistency between each slide.

Placeholders that contain text usually display the prompt "Click to add ..." to help you add text content to a slide. Although placeholders can be formatted differently on each slide, consistent formatting can be achieved by changing placeholder formatting using the Slide Master.

Placeholders can contain text, pictures, tables, charts, SmartArt graphics, and media clips. Users sometimes refer to them as "text boxes," but they are more than just containers for text. Placeholders ensure that the design of an entire presentation is consistent and that positioning and formatting remain the same. Inconsistent formatting between each slide can detract from a presentation's impact.

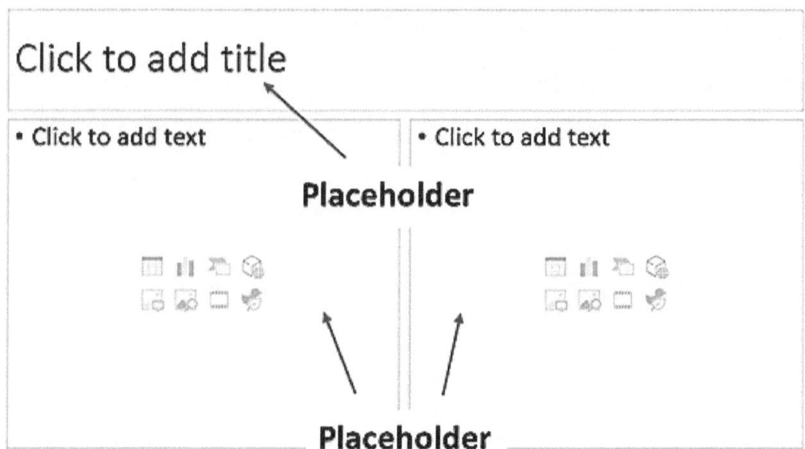

To begin using placeholders in PowerPoint, follow these steps:

- Open Microsoft PowerPoint
- If the Start Screen is displayed, select Blank Presentation. Otherwise, proceed to the next step.

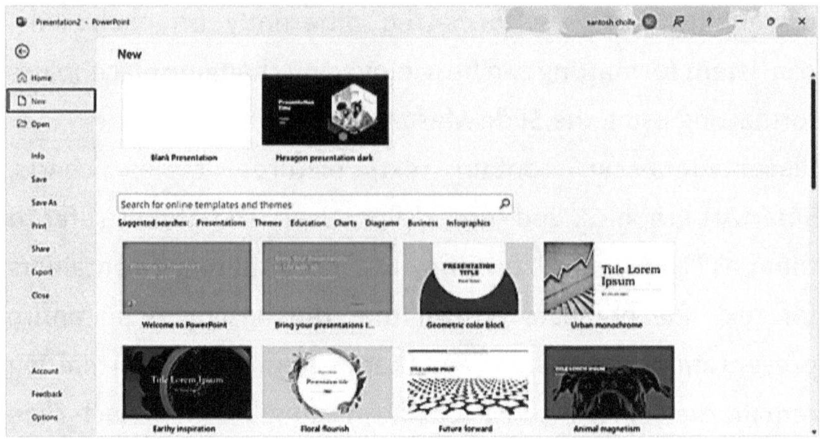

Upon opening a new blank presentation in Microsoft PowerPoint, you will notice that there are two placeholders with prompts to enter text. The first one is the Title placeholder, and the second one is for adding a subheading.

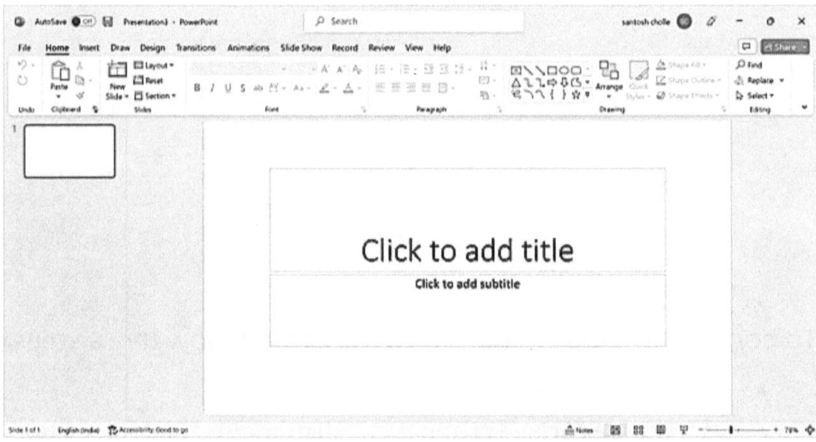

Customizing a Placeholder in PowerPoint

It's common to see users inserting new content onto a slide using the commands on the Ribbon, such as "Insert" > "Picture," even if there are already placeholders on the slide. However, it's important to remember that placeholders can be edited, formatted, resized, and moved on the slide if needed. It's best to use the placeholders already on the slide before adding additional ones or other elements.

To edit or add text to a placeholder:
- Click once anywhere inside the placeholder area with the left mouse button, e.g., inside the first placeholder that says "Click to add title."

- The cursor will now blink, ready for you to enter text.

- Enter your presentation title, such as "Using Placeholders."

- The cursor will continue to blink inside the placeholder until you click outside the placeholder to deselect it.

- Click inside the second placeholder and enter a subtitle, such as your name or a tagline.

- Once you have finished typing, click outside the placeholder to finish editing the text.

If you accidentally press "Enter" (which can happen out of habit), a new paragraph will appear within the placeholder.

Use the "Backspace" key to remove the new paragraph and then click outside the placeholder to deselect it.

To format text within a placeholder:

- Click once inside the placeholder area to display the blinking cursor.

- Use the mouse cursor to highlight the text you wish to format.

- Use the formatting tools on the "Home" tab of the Ribbon to apply any formatting styles.

OR

- To format the entire content of the placeholder at once, place your cursor on the border of the placeholder until you see a four-headed cursor appear.

- Click once with the left mouse button to select the entire placeholder.

- The outside border will now be a solid black line, whereas it was previously a dotted line.

- Utilize the formatting options provided on the Home tab of the Ribbon to apply desired font styles, sizes, or other formatting features.

Resizing a Placeholder:

Once a placeholder is selected, you will notice eight resize handles around its border, as well as a rotation handle. These handles enable you to resize and rotate the placeholder to meet your needs. If you wish to keep placeholder formatting consistent throughout your presentation, it is best to make use of the existing placeholders before adding any new ones.

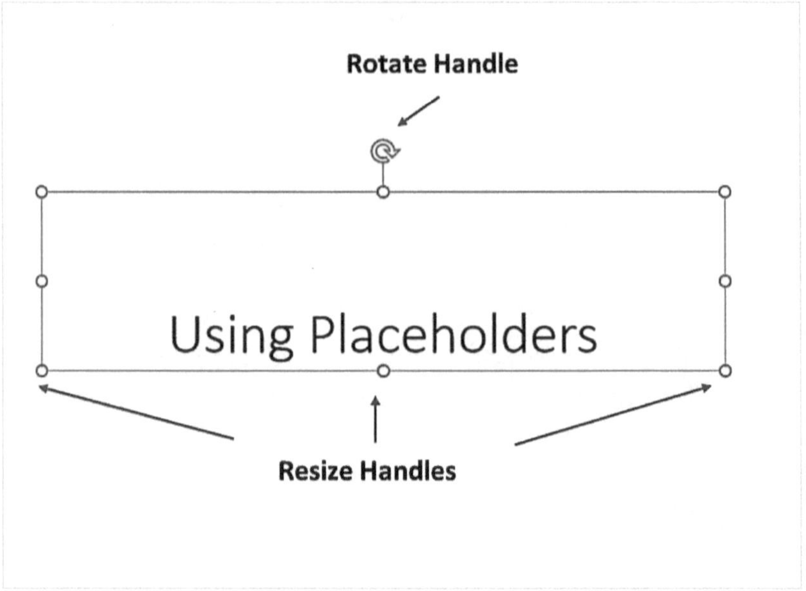

Resizing a placeholder:

- Hover your cursor over the resize handle you want to use.

- The cursor will turn into a two-headed arrow.

- Click and hold the left mouse button and drag it towards the centre or edge of the slide to adjust the size.

-

Rotating a placeholder:

- Position your cursor over the rotate handle located at the top of the placeholder.

- The cursor will turn into a counter clockwise circular arrow.

- Click and hold the left mouse button and move the cursor to the left or right, depending on the desired direction of rotation.

With these resizing and rotating techniques, you can ensure consistency in your placeholders across all your slides. Once you become adept at working with placeholders, you can explore more advanced techniques such as using Slide Masters to create custom templates that suit your needs.

Choosing a slide layout:

PowerPoint's slide layout feature offers pre-designed templates for various types of slides, providing placeholders for text boxes, tables, SmartArt, pictures, and more to contain the content on your slide. These placeholders define the formatting and positioning of the slide's content. Choosing the appropriate slide layout can save significant time as it eliminates the need to create the slide's design from scratch.

The selection of a suitable slide layout is entirely based on the type of content that you want to present. If you cannot find a slide layout that precisely fits your requirements, I suggest choosing the layout that is most similar to what you need. In case none of the available layout options are suitable, you can create a custom layout to fulfil your specific needs, which can then be used in any future presentations.

Below is a list of the available slide layout options, along with a description of their uses.

- **Title Slide**

The purpose of this layout is to create an opening slide where the presentation heading is the main focus. It is designed specifically for this purpose.

- **Title and Content**

This slide layout is widely used and features a title area at the top of the slide, followed by content displayed in bullet points below.

- **Section Header**

If you need to include a new heading that leads to a new topic within your presentation, this layout provides a suitable option. It can be used as a sub-heading slide.

- **Two Content**

The Two Content layout is similar to the Title and Content layout but provides a two-column design for displaying content.

- **Comparison**

This layout is almost identical to the Two Content layout, but it includes a dedicated area at the top of the two-column design for adding a heading.

- **Title Only**

This layout features a title area at the top of the slide but does not include any content area.

- **Blank**

This slide is entirely blank with no pre-defined layout or content.

- **Content with Caption**

This layout offers a design that includes a table, graph, SmartArt, picture, clipart, or media clip along with a caption area that features a title and text.

- **Picture with Caption**

This layout presents a design that includes a picture, along with a caption area featuring a title and text.

The slide layout feature in PowerPoint provides a significant time-saving benefit as you can simply click and start typing information directly into the placeholders. You do not need to create your own text boxes or apply formatting, as the slide layout options display prompts that guide you where to enter information. These prompts may include phrases like "Click to add title," "Click to add subtitle," "Click to add text," and so on. If a placeholder contains elements such as pictures, tables, or SmartArt, you will see icons associated with those types of elements. To insert an element, you simply click on its corresponding icon and choose from the various available options.

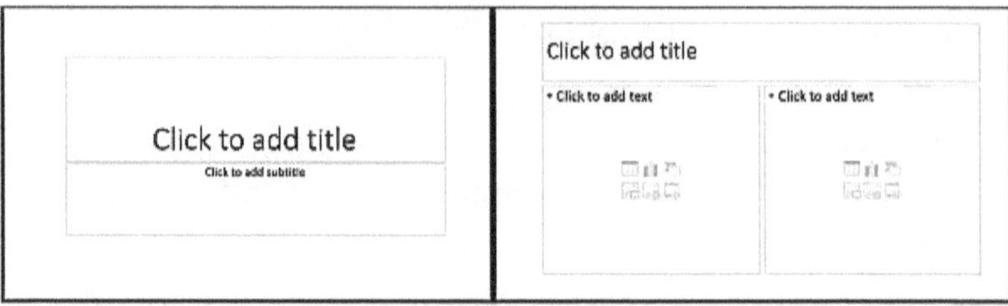

When tasked with reviewing or improving a PowerPoint presentation, I examine various aspects, including design. One common issue I encounter is when users incorrectly set slide layouts on individual slides. A clear example of this can be seen in the image below. The slide may look fine when viewed in slideshow mode, but when viewed in normal view, placeholders and prompts to add text may still be visible on the slide, causing confusion.

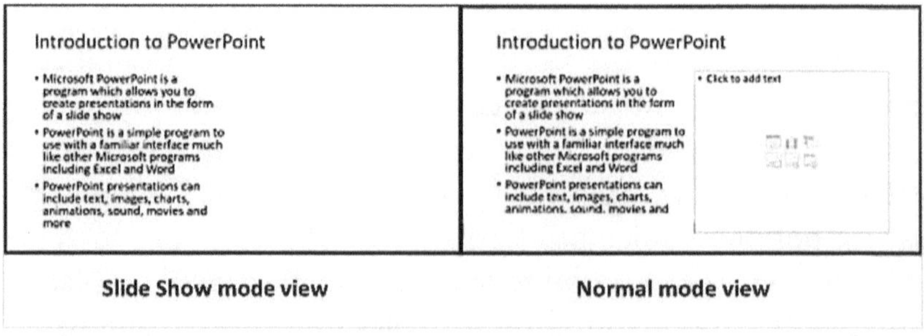

Using an incorrect slide layout can lead to issues down the line, such as problems with text box positioning and animations. It can also result in poorly designed presentations that do not effectively convey information. This issue is particularly significant when multiple people are involved in creating or using the same presentation.

Follow these steps to use the correct slide layout.

- To begin, open Microsoft PowerPoint

- When you open PowerPoint, a new blank slide and a "Title Slide" will appear by default. If you want to make changes to a specific presentation, you can press Ctrl + F12 to open the "Open" dialog box, which will allow you to navigate to and open the desired file.

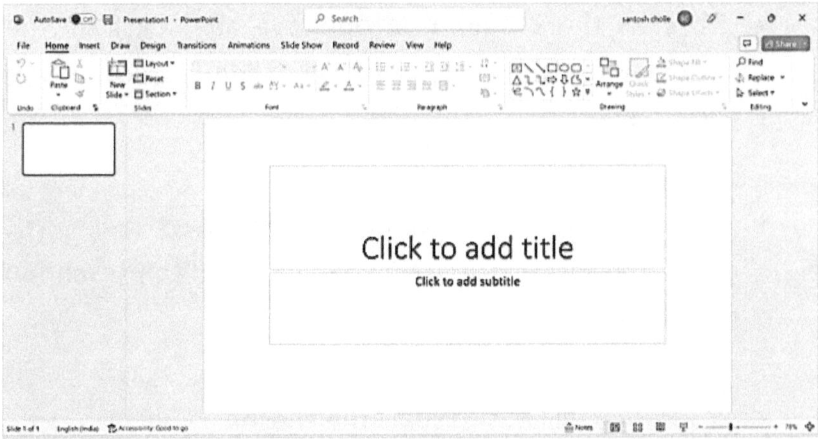

- Next, select the slide that you want to change the slide layout for. If you are working on a new, blank presentation, you can simply change the layout of the first slide.

- Click on the "Layout" button, which you can find in the "Slides" group on the "Home" tab.

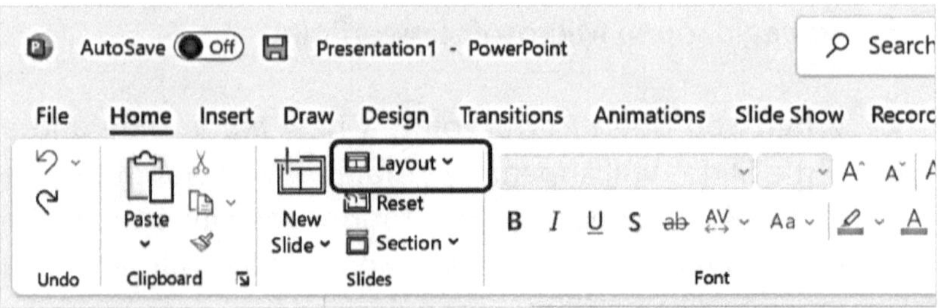

- To view the 9 built-in layouts available, click on the "Layout" button located in the "Slides" group of the "Home" tab.

- You may click on the layout that best suits your needs or is the closest match to what you want to present on the slide.

- Your slide will now display the chosen layout.

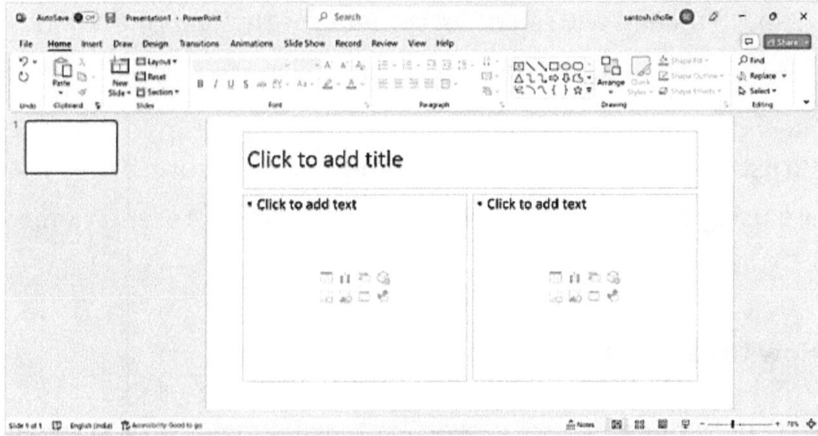

- You should make sure to delete any unused placeholders once you have entered information into the relevant ones.

- To remove a placeholder, click on its outer border and then hit the "Delete" key on your keyboard.

- Proceed with creating content for the rest of the slides in a similar manner as required.

I trust that these tips have been helpful in ensuring that you are using the appropriate slide layout for your presentation.

How to reuse slides in PowerPoint

If you frequently use PowerPoint, you might find yourself wanting to reuse slides from presentations you've created in the past. While many users resort to copying and pasting slides between presentations, it's actually possible to reuse slides in PowerPoint with just a few clicks.

By using the "reuse slides" feature, you can choose to keep the original formatting or apply the formatting used in your new presentation. This technique can save you time when preparing presentations, especially for training sessions. PowerPoint even provides a preview of each slide from your previous presentation, allowing you to insert one, two, or all of them into your new presentation.

Importing slides using the reuse slides feature creates a copy of the original, so you don't need to worry about removing the original slide from its original location.

Reusing slides in PowerPoint can significantly increase your productivity when creating new presentations. Instead of starting from scratch, you can utilize previous slide layouts, images, headings, and content. This technique can also facilitate content sharing across your organization, enabling staff to maintain consistency in messaging and branding.

To reuse slides in PowerPoint, simply follow these steps:

- Open the new presentation where you want to insert the existing slides

- Click the bottom half of the "New Slide" button from the Home tab to display the drop-down menu.

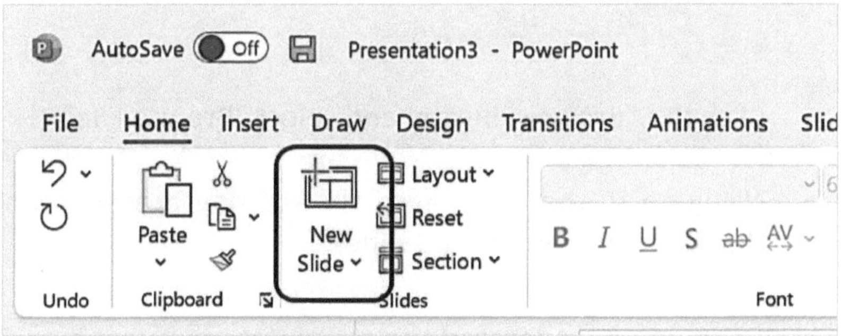

- Next step involves selecting the "Reuse Slides" option from the bottom of the menu.

- This will result in the appearance of the "Reuse Slides" pane.

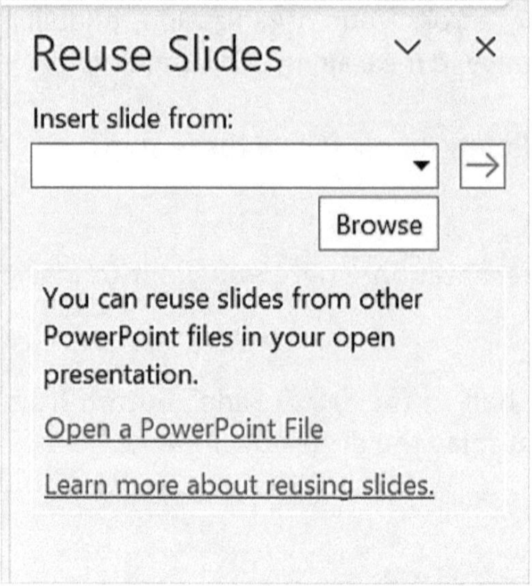

- Click the "Browse" button and select "Browse File".

- Navigate to the location of the existing presentation that contains the desired slides.

- Once you have located the presentation, select it and click "Open" .

- Finally, the slides will be displayed in the pane.

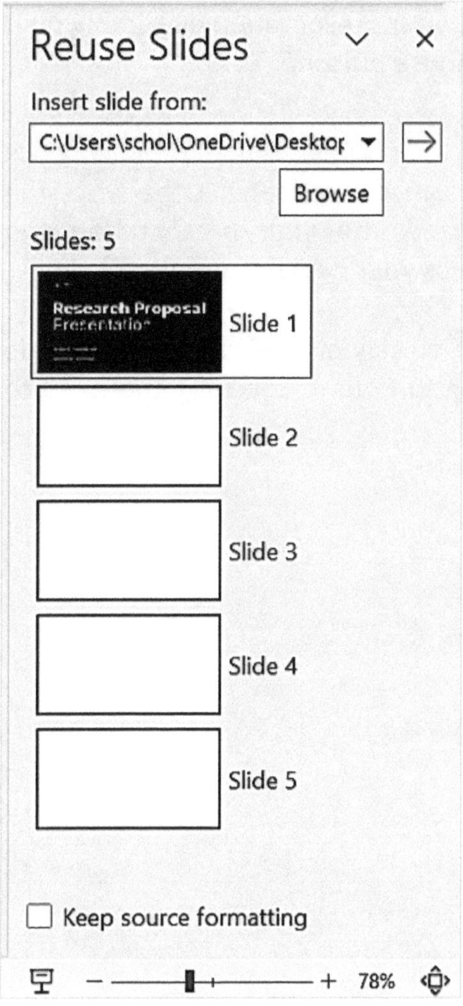

- If you are unsure about or unable to read the content of each slide, simply hover your mouse over the thumbnail to display a larger preview.

- To insert a slide into your presentation by clicking on it once with the left mouse button.

- If you wish to retain the original source formatting tick the box at the bottom of the pane. Otherwise, the slides will be inserted into your presentation and formatted the same as your new presentation's slides.

Using this method, you can quickly and efficiently reuse slide content across multiple presentations, reducing the need to reformat slide information.

9

Common Mistakes and How to Avoid Them

The PowerPoint Edge - Mastering the Art of Storytelling

There are many common mistakes that people make when creating PowerPoint presentations, from using too much text to not practicing their delivery. In this chapter, we will explore these common mistakes, and provide tips and strategies for avoiding them.

While PowerPoint presentations can be a powerful tool for communicating ideas, there are several common mistakes that presenters often make that can detract from the effectiveness of their presentations. Here are some of the most common mistakes and how to avoid them:

Overloading slides with text:

One common mistake in PowerPoint presentations is overloading slides with text. This can make the slides overwhelming and difficult to read, leading to disengagement from the audience. It is important to remember that the slides are there to support the presenter's message, not to replace it. Therefore, it is best to keep the text on each slide to a minimum and use bullet points to highlight key ideas.

To avoid overloading slides with text, presenters can use the rule of six, which suggests limiting the number of bullet points to six per slide and limiting the number of words per bullet point to six. This will help to keep the presentation focused and easy to follow.

Another way to avoid overloading slides with text is to use visuals instead of words to convey the message. This can be done by using images, videos, or diagrams to illustrate key ideas. Visuals can be much more engaging than text, and they can help the audience to better understand and remember the message being presented.

In summary, overloading slides with text is a common mistake in PowerPoint presentations that can be easily avoided by keeping text to a minimum, using bullet points, and incorporating visuals to support the message.

Using low-quality images:

Poor quality images can detract from the effectiveness of your presentation. To avoid this, use high-quality images that are relevant to your message and make sure they are properly formatted and displayed.

Using low-quality images in PowerPoint presentations can significantly reduce the effectiveness of the visual aid. Images that are blurry, pixelated, or distorted can be distracting and difficult to understand, making it harder for the audience to engage with the content being presented.

To avoid using low-quality images, it's important to use high-resolution images that are relevant to the presentation topic. It's recommended to use royalty-free images or create original images or graphics for the presentation. This can ensure that the images are not only high-quality but also unique to the presentation, making it more memorable for the audience.

If low-quality images must be used due to technical limitations or time constraints, it's essential to optimize the image for the presentation. This can include resizing the image to fit the slide, adjusting the brightness and contrast, and cropping the image to highlight the relevant details.

Overall, using high-quality images in PowerPoint presentations can enhance the audience's understanding and engagement with the content, while low-quality images can have the opposite effect. Therefore, it's essential to use appropriate images that are of high quality and relevant to the presentation topic.

Using too many animations:

While animations can be useful in emphasizing key points, using too many can be distracting and confusing. Limit your use of animations and make sure they are relevant to your message.

Using too many animations in PowerPoint can be distracting for the audience and may take away from the overall message of the presentation. While animations can be useful for emphasizing certain points or adding visual interest to a slide, overusing them can result in a cluttered and confusing presentation.

It is important to use animations judiciously and purposefully. Animations should enhance the content of the presentation, not distract from it. For example, using a simple fade-in animation to bring up a bullet point can help draw attention to the point and make it more memorable, while using a complex animation sequence that takes several seconds to complete may be more distracting than helpful.

When using animations, it is also important to consider the timing and duration of the animation. Animations that are too slow or too fast can be difficult for the audience to follow, while animations that last too long can cause the audience to lose interest.

Overall, the key is to use animations in a way that adds value to the presentation without detracting from the message. A good rule of thumb is to use animations sparingly, focusing on simple and subtle effects that help emphasize key points and improve the overall flow and visual appeal of the presentation.

Using a confusing or unprofessional design:

The design of your presentation can have a big impact on how it is received. Avoid using overly complex or confusing designs, and make sure your presentation has a professional and cohesive look and feel.

Using a confusing or unprofessional design in PowerPoint can hinder the effectiveness of your presentation. Your design should be consistent, visually appealing, and relevant to your topic. Here are some tips to avoid using a confusing or unprofessional design:

- **Stick to a consistent colour scheme:** Choose a colour scheme that complements your brand or topic, and use it consistently throughout your presentation. Avoid using too many colours or clashing colour combinations that make it difficult for your audience to read your slides.

- **Use legible fonts:** Choose a font that is easy to read and use it consistently throughout your presentation. Avoid using multiple fonts or decorative fonts that can be difficult to read.

- **Keep it simple:** Avoid cluttering your slides with too much text, images, or animations. Keep your design simple and clean, with plenty of white space.

- **Use high-quality images:** Low-quality images can make your presentation look unprofessional. Use high-quality images that are relevant to your topic and enhance your message.

- **Avoid using too many animations:** While animations can add visual interest to your presentation, too many can be distracting and detract from your message. Use animations sparingly and only when they add value to your presentation.

By following these tips, you can create a professional and effective design for your PowerPoint presentation.

Failing to practice:

One of the biggest mistakes presenters make is failing to practice their presentation. This can result in a lack of confidence and clarity during the actual presentation. Make sure to practice your presentation several times to become comfortable with the material and the flow of the presentation.

Failing to practice is a common mistake that can significantly impact the quality of a presentation in PowerPoint. Practicing allows the presenter to become familiar with the material and the flow of the presentation, leading to a more confident delivery. Without practice, the presenter may stumble over their words or forget important points, leading to a less engaging and less effective presentation.

Additionally, practicing allows the presenter to identify and address any issues with the presentation, such as technical difficulties or confusing language. By practicing, the presenter can make necessary changes to ensure that the presentation is as clear and effective as possible.

It is important to note that practicing does not mean simply running through the presentation once or twice. Ideally, the presenter should practice multiple times, making adjustments and refinements as necessary to ensure that the presentation is polished and effective. Practice can also include getting feedback from others, such as colleagues or friends, to identify areas for improvement.

Failing to practice can also lead to the presenter relying too heavily on the PowerPoint slides rather than engaging with the audience. By practicing, the presenter can become more comfortable with the material and better able to engage with the audience, resulting in a more effective presentation overall.

Ignoring the audience:

Presenters often make the mistake of ignoring their audience and failing to engage with them. To avoid this, make sure to engage with your audience throughout your presentation, ask questions, and encourage discussion.

Ignoring the audience is a common mistake presenters make in PowerPoint presentations. It's essential to keep your audience in mind while preparing your presentation and during the actual delivery. Failing to do so can result in a disengaged audience, making it challenging to deliver your message effectively.

Ignoring the audience can manifest in several ways, such as failing to consider their needs and preferences, not adapting to their level of understanding or interest, and not responding to their questions or feedback. To avoid these mistakes, consider the following tips:

- **Know your audience:** Before creating your presentation, research and understand your audience's background, interests, and expectations. Tailor your message to their level of understanding and use language and examples that resonate with them.

- **Engage your audience:** Keep your audience engaged by asking questions, using humour, and involving them in activities or discussions. This will help you gauge their level of understanding and adapt your message accordingly.

- **Address their concerns:** Be mindful of your audience's concerns and address them in your presentation. Acknowledge any potential objections or questions they may have and provide clear and concise answers.

- **Respond to feedback:** Encourage feedback from your audience and be open to criticism. Respond to their comments and questions promptly, and be willing to adjust your presentation if necessary.

By avoiding the mistake of ignoring your audience, you can create a more effective and engaging PowerPoint presentation that resonates with your audience and achieves your desired outcome.

Going over time:

Going over time can be frustrating for the audience and can result in them disengaging from the presentation. To avoid this, make sure to stick to your allotted time and pace your presentation accordingly.

Going over time during a presentation can be a major mistake in PowerPoint. It's important to stick to the allotted time for your presentation, as going over time can cause your audience to lose interest or become frustrated. It's important to practice your presentation ahead of time to ensure that you can deliver it within the time frame given to you.

If you find yourself running out of time, it's important to be flexible and adjust your presentation accordingly. You may need to cut out certain sections or condense your material to ensure that you can cover the most important points within the allotted time. On the other hand, if you find that you have extra time, it's important not to fill it with unnecessary information or rambling. Instead, you can use the extra time to engage your audience with questions or to provide more detail on key points.

In short, being mindful of time and staying within your allotted time frame is crucial to delivering a successful presentation in PowerPoint.

Overall, avoiding these common mistakes can help you deliver a more effective and engaging PowerPoint presentation. By focusing on concise text, high-quality images, relevant animations, professional design, practicing your presentation, engaging with your audience, and sticking to your allotted time, you can deliver a presentation that effectively communicates your message and resonates with your audience.

10

Tips and Tricks for Creating Great PowerPoint Presentations

Finally, in this chapter, we will provide some additional tips and tricks for creating great PowerPoint presentations. These include how to create effective slide titles, how to use storytelling to engage your audience, and how to incorporate multimedia.

Creating an effective PowerPoint presentation involves careful planning, design, and delivery. Here are some tips and tricks for creating great PowerPoint presentations:

Start with a clear outline:

Before you begin creating your PowerPoint, create an outline that highlights the key points you want to cover. Think about the purpose of your presentation, who your audience is, and what message you want to convey.

Starting with a clear outline is essential for creating an effective and well-organized PowerPoint presentation. An outline is a plan that provides a structure for your presentation, including the main points you want to cover, the order in which you want to cover them, and any supporting information or details.

When creating your outline, it's important to consider the purpose of your presentation, your audience, and the key messages you want to convey. You can start by identifying the main topics or themes you want to cover, then break them down into more specific subtopics or points. Each point in your outline should be concise, clear, and relevant to your audience.

Your outline should also include an introduction that grabs the attention of your audience and sets the stage for your presentation. This can be done through a compelling story, a surprising fact or statistic, a quote, or a question that engages your audience.

Finally, your outline should include a conclusion that summarizes your main points and provides a clear call-to-action or takeaway for your audience. This could be a final statement, a question for reflection or discussion, or a suggestion for further reading or resources.

Starting with a clear outline helps ensure that your PowerPoint presentation is well-organized, easy to follow, and engaging for your audience. It can also help you stay on track and avoid going off-topic during your presentation.

Keep it simple

Avoid overloading your presentation with too much information, complex graphics, or too many slides. Instead, focus on a few key points and use clear and concise language.

Keeping your presentation simple is one of the most important principles of creating effective PowerPoint presentations. When creating a presentation, it's important to remember that the slides are not the presentation themselves but rather a visual aid to support and enhance your message. The following are some tips to help you keep it simple:

- **Limit the number of slides:** Your presentation should have a clear structure and flow, and you should avoid overloading your audience with too much information.

Limit your presentation to the essential points you want to make.

- **Use simple and clear language:** Avoid using complex language, jargon, or acronyms that may be unfamiliar to your audience. Use simple, clear language that is easy to understand.

- **Use visuals to support your message:** Use visuals like images, charts, and graphs to support your message and help your audience understand your points. Visuals can be more effective than text in conveying information.

- **Use a consistent design:** Choose a consistent design for your presentation, including fonts, colours, and formatting. This helps to create a professional and polished look for your presentation.

- **Use white space:** Don't overcrowd your slides with too much information. Leave some white space to make your presentation easier to read and less cluttered.

Keeping your presentation simple can help ensure that your message is clear and that your audience is engaged and attentive.

Use high-quality images:

Adding relevant images to your slides can help to grab your audience's attention and make your presentation more engaging. Be sure to use high-quality images that are relevant to the content on the slide.

Using high-quality images in your PowerPoint presentation can significantly enhance its visual appeal and impact. High-quality images can grab the audience's attention, convey information more effectively, and make the presentation more memorable.

Here are some tips for using high-quality images in your PowerPoint presentation:

- **Choose relevant images:** Use images that are relevant to your presentation topic and help reinforce the message you are trying to convey.

- **Use high-resolution images:** Low-resolution images can appear pixelated and unprofessional, so it's essential to use high-resolution images. If you are using images from the internet, make sure to use ones that are at least 1920 pixels wide by 1080 pixels tall for HD presentations.

- **Crop and resize images:** Crop images to focus on the most important elements, and resize them to fit the slide without distorting the aspect ratio.

- **Use a consistent style:** Use images that have a consistent style, such as colour or composition, to create a cohesive look throughout the presentation.

- **Use stock photos judiciously:** Stock photos can be useful, but try to avoid using generic or cliché images. Use high-quality, original images wherever possible.

- **Use image captions:** Adding captions to your images can provide additional context and make the information easier to understand.

Remember that using high-quality images is not just about aesthetics; it also makes your presentation more effective in conveying your message.

Use consistent design:

Consistent design throughout your PowerPoint presentation helps to create a cohesive and professional look. Use the same fonts, colours, and background on all slides.

Using consistent design in PowerPoint is important for creating a professional and visually appealing presentation. This means that all the slides in your presentation should have a similar look and feel, including the use of colours, fonts, graphics, and other design elements. Consistency helps to make your presentation easier to follow and understand, as well as more aesthetically pleasing.

To achieve consistent design, you can start by selecting a theme or template for your presentation that includes the fonts, colours, and design elements you want to use throughout. You can then apply this theme or template to all your slides, ensuring that each slide has a consistent look and feel.

It's also important to use the same design principles throughout your presentation, such as the placement of text and images, the use of white space, and the alignment of elements. This helps to create a sense of unity and cohesion throughout your presentation.

Consistent design not only makes your presentation more visually appealing but also helps to reinforce your message and makes it easier for your audience to follow along. By keeping a consistent design throughout your presentation, you can make sure that your message is clear and effective, and that your audience stays engaged throughout.

Use animations and transitions sparingly:

While animations and transitions can add visual interest to your presentation, too much can be distracting. Use them sparingly and only when they help to illustrate your point.

When creating a PowerPoint presentation, it can be tempting to add lots of animations and transitions to make the slides look more dynamic and interesting. However, it is important to use animations and transitions sparingly to avoid overwhelming the audience and detracting from the content of the presentation.

Animations should be used to enhance the content of the slide and not just for the sake of adding animation. For example, animations can be used to highlight specific points or to show how processes work. Transitions should also be used sparingly and should be simple and subtle to avoid distracting the audience.

Additionally, it is important to use consistent animations and transitions throughout the presentation. Using a consistent style helps to create a sense of coherence and professionalism in the presentation.

Overall, the key is to use animations and transitions in moderation, and to ensure they are consistent and add value to the presentation rather than detracting from it.

Use data visualization tools:

When presenting data, use graphs, charts, and other visual tools to make the data more understandable and memorable.

Data visualization is a powerful tool for presenting complex information in a clear and concise manner. In PowerPoint, there are several data visualization tools available that can help you convey your message more effectively.

One of the most common data visualization tools in PowerPoint is charts and graphs. These tools can be used to display numerical data in a way that is easy to understand. For example, a bar chart can be used to show how different products or services compare in terms of sales or revenue. A line graph can be used to show how a particular variable changes over time.

In addition to charts and graphs, PowerPoint also includes tools for creating infographics. Infographics are visual representations of data or information that are designed to be both informative and visually appealing. They can be used to illustrate a process, explain a concept, or present a large amount of information in a single graphic.

Another data visualization tool in PowerPoint is the SmartArt graphic. SmartArt graphics are pre-designed diagrams that can be used to illustrate relationships, processes, and hierarchies. They are easy to customize and can be used to convey complex information in a visually appealing way.

Overall, using data visualization tools in PowerPoint can help you create more effective and engaging presentations. By presenting information in a clear and visually appealing way, you can better capture your audience's attention and convey your message more effectively.

Practice your delivery:

Finally, practice delivering your PowerPoint presentation before the actual presentation. This will help you to feel more confident and comfortable with the material and delivery.

It's important to practice your delivery when presenting data in Excel, just as it is in PowerPoint. Here are some tips to help you practice effectively:

- **Start by reviewing your data:** and determining the key points you want to make. This will help you structure your presentation.

- **Use charts and graphs**: to help visualize your data. Excel has many built-in options for creating charts and graphs, so choose the one that best represents your data and helps you tell your story.

- **Practice presenting your data**: to someone who is unfamiliar with it. This will help you identify areas that may need further explanation and ensure that you are able to convey your message clearly.

- **Time yourself**: to ensure that your presentation fits within the allotted time. This will help you pace yourself during the actual presentation and avoid going over time.

- **Consider recording yourself:** presenting your data so you can review it later and make any necessary adjustments. This will also help you become more comfortable with presenting in Excel.

By following these tips and practicing your delivery, you'll be well-prepared to present your data effectively in Excel.

Here's an example of how to use these tips and tricks to create a great PowerPoint presentation:

Let's say you're giving a presentation to your colleagues about a new project you're working on. You might create an outline that highlights the project's goals, the challenges you've faced, and your proposed solutions.

To keep your presentation simple, you might focus on a few key points and use clear and concise language. You could use high-quality images of the project's progress to help engage your audience and illustrate your points.

To create a consistent design, you might use the same font and colour scheme throughout your presentation. You could use animations and transitions sparingly to help illustrate your points, and use data visualization tools to present data in a clear and understandable way.

Finally, you would practice delivering your PowerPoint presentation before the actual presentation to ensure that you feel confident and comfortable with the material and delivery.

11

Formatting and SmartArt

How to use the Format Painter to copy formatting

Microsoft programs offer some basic clipboard options, including Cut, Copy, and Paste functions that most users are familiar with. However, many users are unaware of the fourth function called Format Painter.

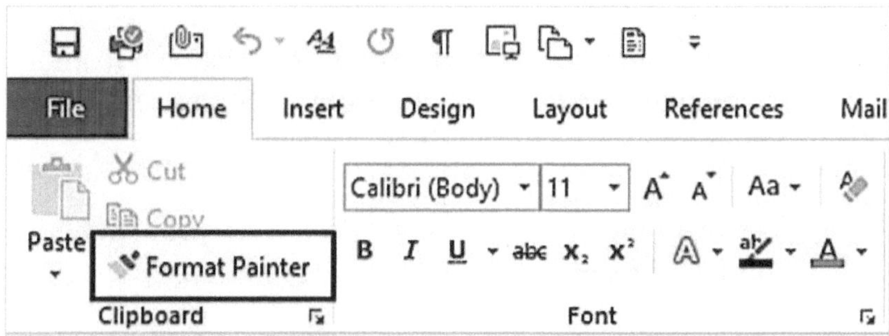

Format Painter is a convenient and efficient tool that enables users to quickly copy formatting from one location to another, eliminating the need to format text multiple times.

With Format Painter, you can copy font style, size, colour, and other text characteristics, but not the actual text itself. If you come across a document with a certain look that you like, you can easily replicate it using this feature. This is particularly useful when working with documents created by someone else, as it allows you to quickly apply formatting to headings or text within the same document or even across to a new document.

Although this example focuses on using Format Painter in Microsoft Word, the process is the same in Excel and

PowerPoint. You can even use Format Painter when creating email messages in Outlook.

Here's how to use Format Painter:

- Open Microsoft Word.

- Type in some sample text or open an existing document that you would like to experiment with. Use Ctrl+F12 to launch the Open dialog box.

- For example, you can type in a list of your favourite features of Word.

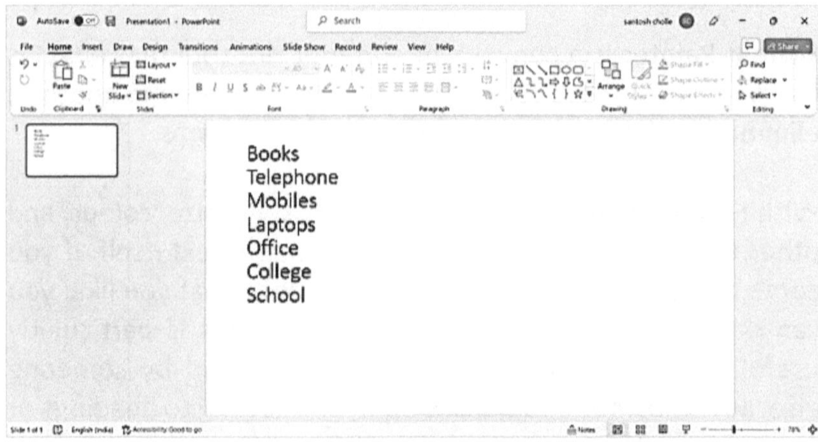

- Next, I'll format the first heading by changing the font style, size, colour, making it bold, underlining it, and centering it on the page.

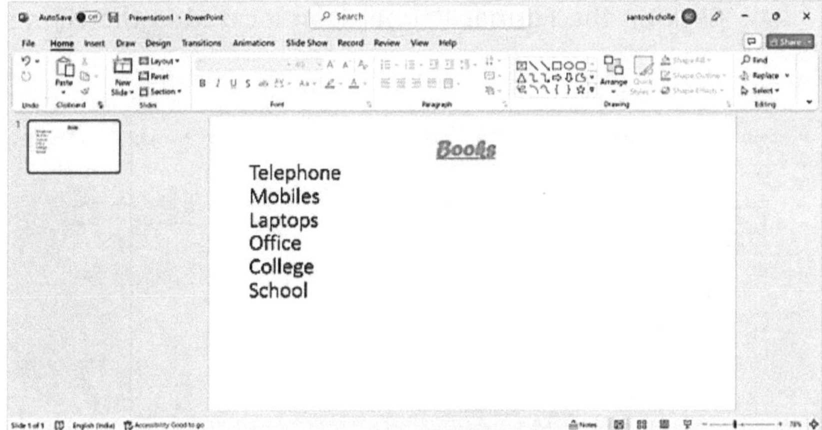

- Now, format the second heading using different formatting options but keep the text left-aligned.

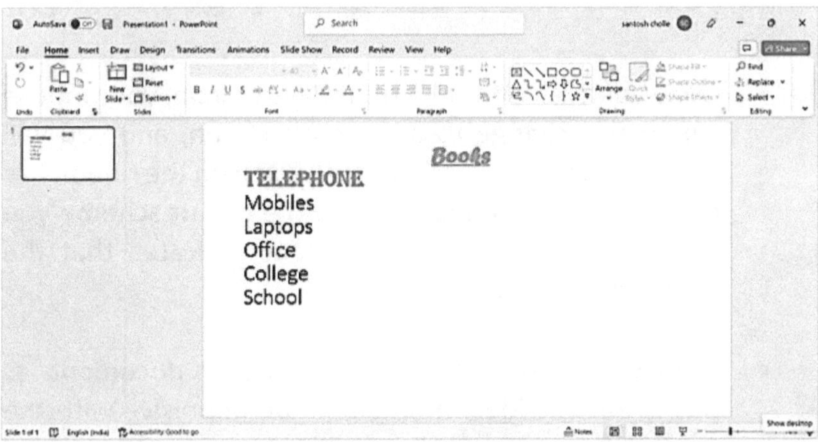

- Next, we will copy the formatting from the first two headings and apply it to the remaining headings.

- Start by selecting the first heading you formatted.

- Click on the Format Painter icon located in the Home tab.

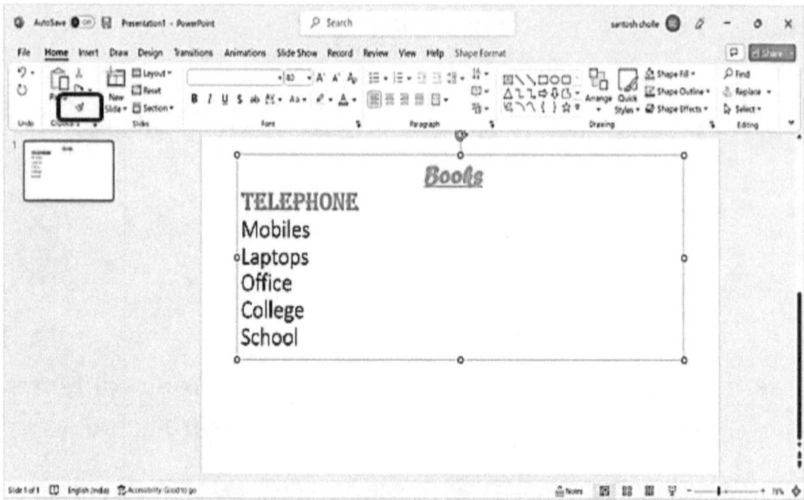

- Once you click on the Format Painter icon, your mouse cursor will change to a paintbrush icon, and you will notice that the Format Painter button on the ribbon has changed colour (depending on the colour scheme you are using). This change in colour indicates that the function is now active.

- Exercise caution while clicking on your document, as this is not the ideal moment to be impulsive with the mouse. Your next click will dictate where the copied formatting is applied.

- Select the third heading and release the mouse button.

- The third heading will now have the same formatting as the first heading, and the button on the Ribbon will revert to its initial colour to indicate that the function is no longer active.

- Repeat this procedure to copy the formatting from the second heading to the fourth heading.

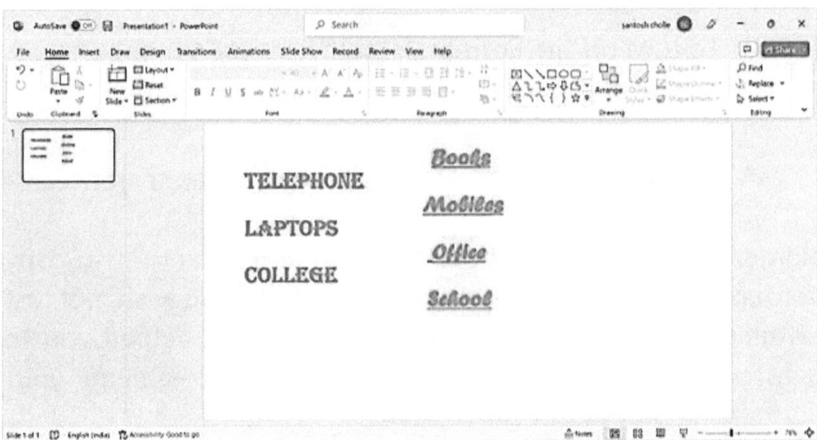

Apply formatting to multiple selections at once

This segment explains how to apply formatting to multiple selections at once using the Format Painter feature. By "locking" this feature, you can apply the same formatting to several headings, sentences, or paragraphs at once.

- To get started, add some plain text headings.

- Select the first one, and click the Format Painter button.

- This time, use a double-click to activate the feature, which will remain active even after formatting the first piece of text.

- Format all five headings, one at a time, until they are all formatted.

- To turn off the Format Painter feature, either press Esc on the keyboard or click the button once more.

- The button should return to its normal appearance.

Remember, you can use the Format Painter feature to copy formatting within any program or document you wish, not just within the same file. Hopefully, this post has helped you to master the Format Painter feature and streamline your formatting process.

Convert text to SmartArt in PowerPoint

When it comes to creating presentations using Microsoft PowerPoint, it's quite common to come across slides that consist of a heading and a list of bullet points or numbered items. However, let's face it - these types of presentations can often turn out to be dull and unengaging. Fortunately, there is an easy way to spruce up your presentation - by using SmartArt graphics. By converting your existing text to SmartArt, you can present your content in various layouts, including lists, cycles, and many more, thus giving your presentation a professional and engaging look.

SmartArt works well with lists, and can also incorporate headings, subheadings, and images. Check out the sample below for a glimpse of the different SmartArt layout options available.

Transforming your text into SmartArt is a quick and easy process that eliminates the need for retyping information. Moreover, SmartArt offers a vast selection of layouts to choose from. It's worth noting that you can effortlessly switch between different layouts and utilize the SmartArt Tools to make various modifications, such as adjusting the colour scheme, adding more Shapes, applying 3D effects, and more.

To convert your text to a SmartArt graphic, you can follow these simple steps:

- Launch Microsoft PowerPoint.

- To open an existing presentation, press Ctrl + O, and the Open dialog box will appear. Navigate to and select the file, then click Open. Alternatively, create a sample slide containing approximately 4-6 bullet points.

- Select the bullet points or text that you want to convert.

- Go to the Home tab and click on the Convert to SmartArt button.

- Another option is to right-click on the selected bullet points and choose "Convert to SmartArt" from the context menu.

- A gallery of available SmartArt graphics should now be displayed:

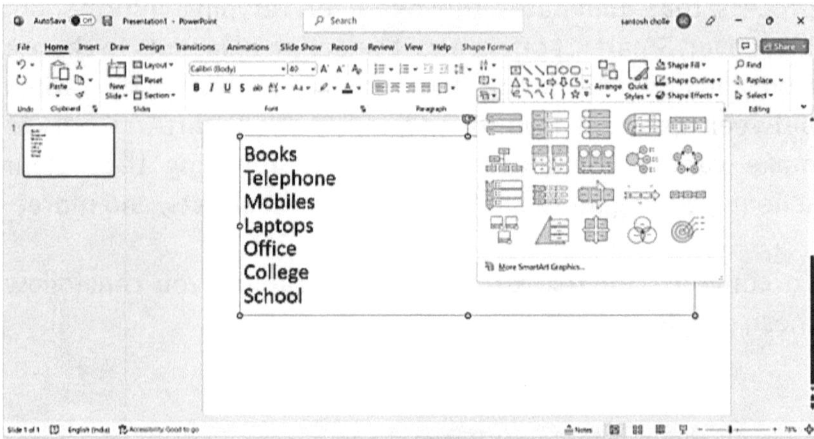

- As you hover your mouse over each SmartArt sample, you will get a live preview of the text on the slide displayed in the background in the chosen SmartArt layout. This preview feature lets you determine if the layout is suitable without actually applying the change.

- When you have found a suitable SmartArt layout, click on it to apply it to your selected text.

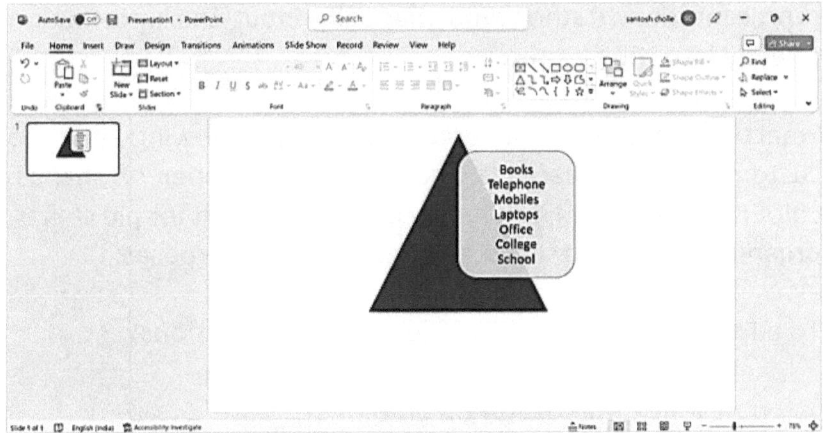

- Once you have converted your text to a SmartArt graphic, you can edit it by selecting the graphic and accessing the SmartArt Tools tab in the ribbon.

How to insert a SmartArt graphic in PowerPoint

Using graphics to represent content can greatly enhance the meaning and visual appeal of any presentation. In my experience, graphics can effectively convey information in a way that a text-filled screen cannot. That's why I appreciate the use of SmartArt. However, like any feature in Microsoft Office, it should be used in moderation. Including too many SmartArt graphics in a presentation with multiple slides may not be beneficial. But, when used appropriately, SmartArt can visually represent your information in the best way possible.

It's common for users to confuse SmartArt with the Charts feature, which is frequently used in Excel and other applications. However, SmartArt is solely graphics-based and doesn't rely on data in the document to create a visual representation. Rather, you manually input the information directly into the graphic.

SmartArt offers tremendous flexibility, allowing you to customize its appearance, including the number of shapes, colour schemes, and more. I've utilized SmartArt for pie charts, organizational charts, and a variety of other purposes.

To add a SmartArt graphic, follow these instructions:

- Launch Microsoft PowerPoint.

- A Title Slide will appear on a new blank presentation.

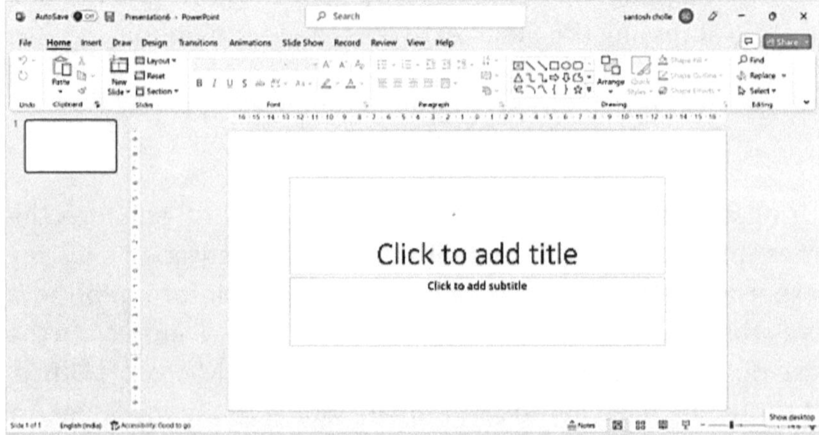

- Let's create a new slide where we can add the SmartArt graphic.

- Click on the New Slide button in the Home tab, and select the Title and Content slide layout, or press Ctrl + M on the keyboard.

- The second slide will now be visible.

- You can add your own title at the top of the slide, such as "My SmartArt ".

- Within the Content area of the slide, you'll see six content options. One of them is the SmartArt graphic icon. Click on it to insert a new SmartArt graphic.

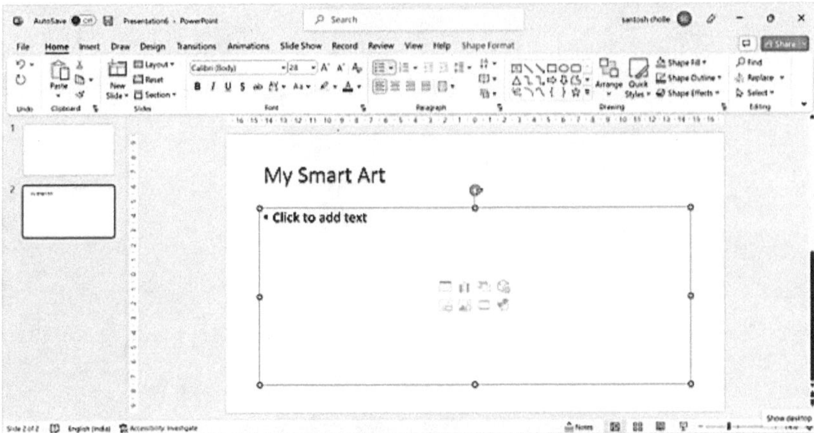

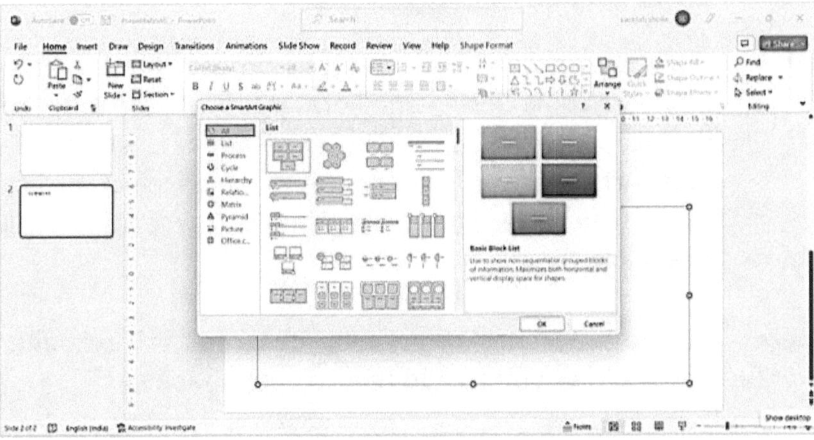

- On the left side of the dialog box, you'll notice the different categories.

- Take a moment to browse through the options, and then choose the Hierarchy category. From there, select the Hierarchy option and click OK.

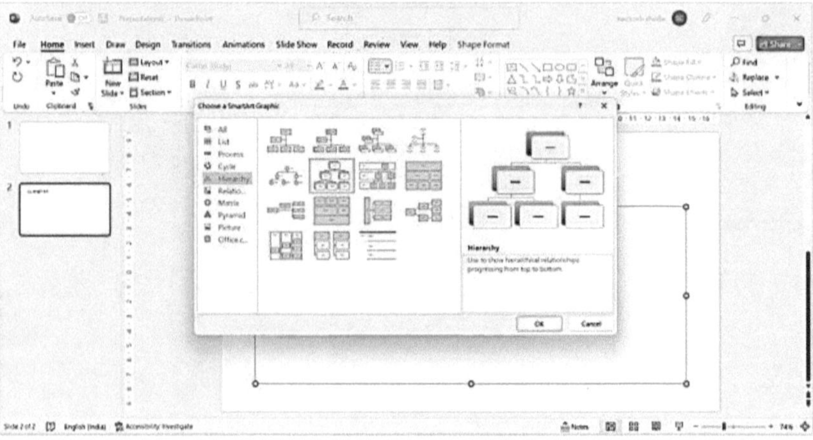

- The SmartArt graphic has been successfully inserted.

- You'll now notice two new tabs on the Ribbon - the SmartArt Tools Design and Format tabs. These tabs are context-sensitive, and will only appear when the SmartArt graphic is selected. Once you deselect or click away from the SmartArt graphic, these tabs will disappear.

- Next to the SmartArt graphic, you'll see the Text pane, which allows you to add text to each shape.

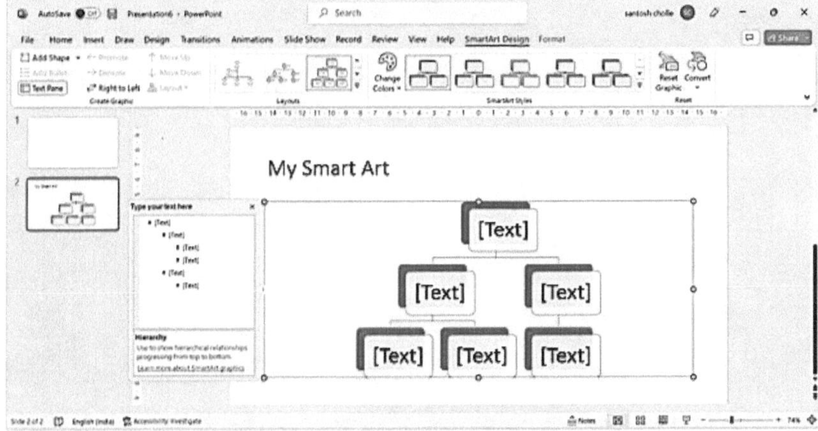

- Instead of using the Text Pane, you can also type directly into the SmartArt graphic shapes.

- To begin, click on the first bullet point in the Text Pane, which represents the highest shape in the hierarchy.

- Enter the desired text. For instance, if you're creating an organizational chart, type in the relevant information.

- Click on the next bullet point, and add text for that shape.

- Continue this process to add text for each shape within the SmartArt graphic.

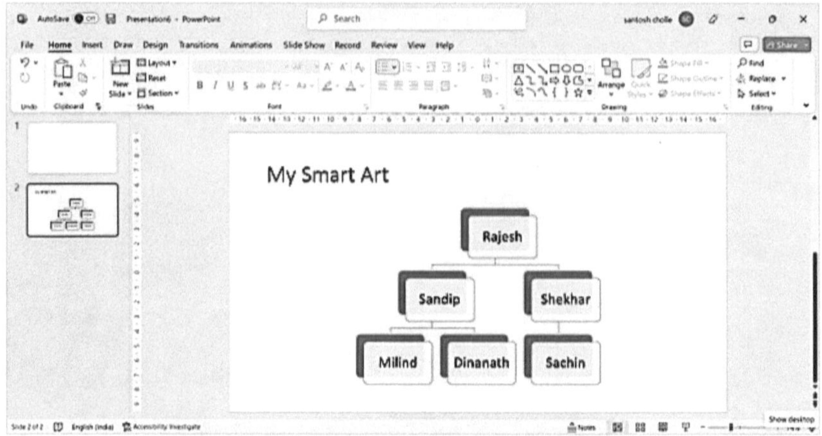

- Suppose we need to include an additional person who reports to Shekhar, but there's only one shape displayed beneath his name.

- To add a new shape, select the shape for Shekhar, or choose his name from the bulleted list if you're using the Task Pane.

- Click on the SmartArt Tools > Design tab.

- Press the Add Shape button, and choose the option Add Shape Below.

- A new shape will now appear, enabling you to add another member to the SmartArt graphic.

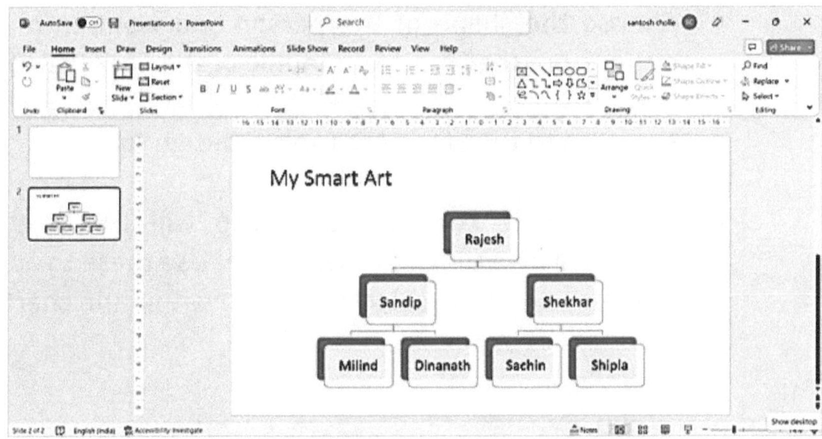

- When using the Task Pane, move your cursor to the end of the previous person's name, and hit the Enter key.

- Similar to how it generates a new bullet point in other Microsoft Office applications, it will create a new shape in this case, enabling you to add another person to the SmartArt graphic.

Moving people around the SmartArt

I often receive a common query during my training sessions about how to reposition individuals within an organizational chart. With changes in job roles, promotions, or shifts in departments, it becomes necessary to move people around. Fortunately, SmartArt provides a simple solution that doesn't involve deleting and recreating their shapes.

Here's how you can move someone within the chart:

- Choose the shape of the person you want to move, either from the SmartArt graphic or the Task Pane list.

- Navigate to the SmartArt Tools > Design tab.

- In the Create Graphic group, you will find buttons labelled Move Up and Move Down. Use these to adjust the position of the selected person within the chart.

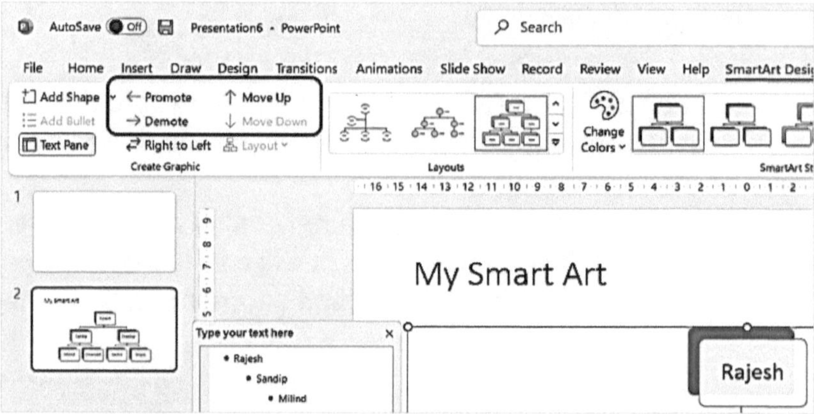

- To adjust the level of someone who has been promoted or demoted, use the "Promote" and "Demote" buttons located in the SmartArt Tools > Design tab. This will change the position of their bullet point within the Task Pane.

I trust that this guide on inserting and manipulating SmartArt graphics in PowerPoint has been helpful.

12

Animation & Transition

How to add slide transitions in PowerPoint

PowerPoint can be overwhelming due to its numerous features, but one of the easiest ways to add some style to your presentation is by using slide transitions.

Slide transitions give your presentation a nice flow by adding an animation effect to slides as they move from one to the next. Whether you want to apply a transition to one slide or all, the process is simple.

Here's how to apply a slide transition in PowerPoint:

- Open PowerPoint and the presentation you want to work on.

- Select the first slide you want to apply the transition to.

- Click on the Transitions tab located in the Ribbon.

- You'll now see a gallery of transitions displayed, and there are lots to choose from.

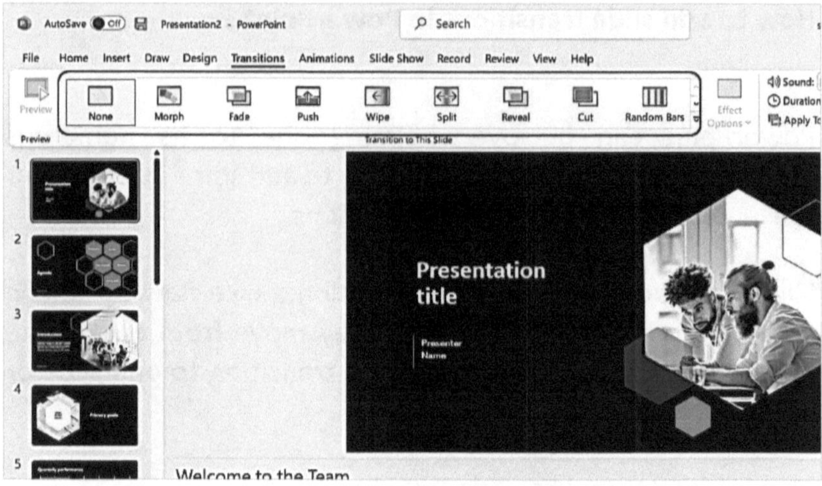

To apply a slide transition in PowerPoint, first, open the presentation you want to work with and select the first slide.

- Click on the Transitions tab in the Ribbon, and you will see a gallery of transitions displayed.

- Hover your mouse over any of the transition types, such as Push, Split, or Reveal, to see a preview of the transition effect on the screen.

- Click on the desired transition to apply it to the current slide.

- A star symbol will appear under the slide number in the navigation pane on the left of the screen.

- Repeat the process for other slides you want to add transitions to.

To preview the slide transition:

- Select the Slide Show tab from the Ribbon, and choose to run the slideshow either from the beginning or from the current slide.

- Slide transitions provide a nice movement or flow to your presentation and can be applied to one or all slides.

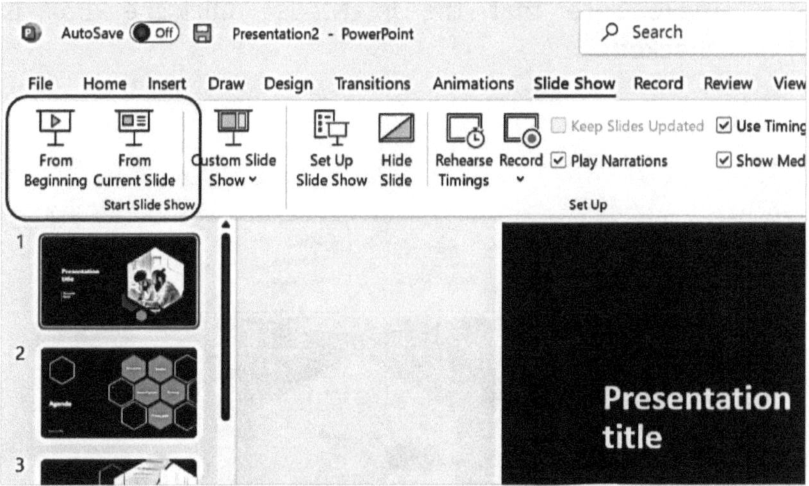

- Make sure that you have selected the slide to which you want to apply the timing adjustment for the slide transition.

- Go to the Transitions tab on the Ribbon if you are not already there.

- On the right side of the transition gallery, you will see the Timing group.

- Use the Duration drop-down menu to set the desired time for the slide transition. The default duration is 1 second.

- If you want the slide to transition automatically, make sure that the On Mouse Click checkbox is unchecked.

- If you want to manually control the slide transition, make sure that the On Mouse Click checkbox is checked.

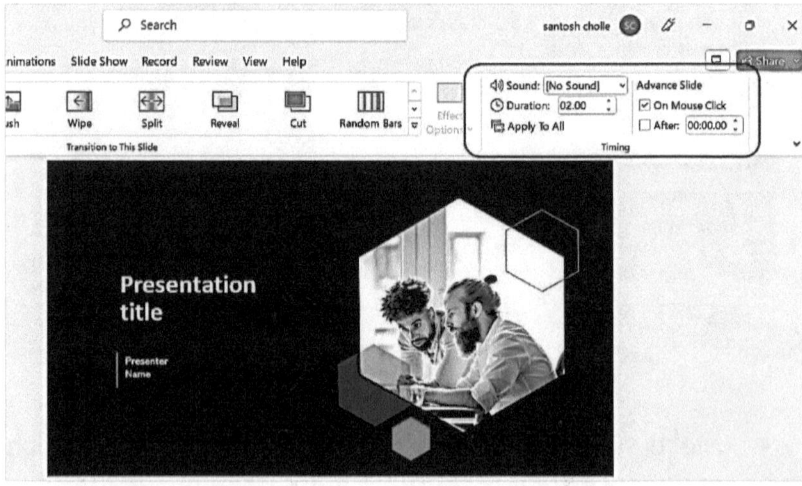

The Duration setting can be found in the Timing group, and in my case, it is set to 02.00 (2 seconds). 4. Adjust the Duration setting higher or lower, depending on whether you want to speed up or slow down the transition effect.

Using the same transition for all slides

Sometimes, people tend to get too carried away with slide transitions and apply a different one to every slide in their presentation, which can make the audience feel dizzy. To avoid overdoing it, you can use the same slide transition for all slides.

If your presentation has a large number of slides, it would be tedious to apply the transition to each slide manually. Here's how you can apply the same transition to all slides at once:

- Ensure that you are satisfied with the slide transition and timing that you have applied to the slide.

- Click on the Apply to All button in the Timing group.

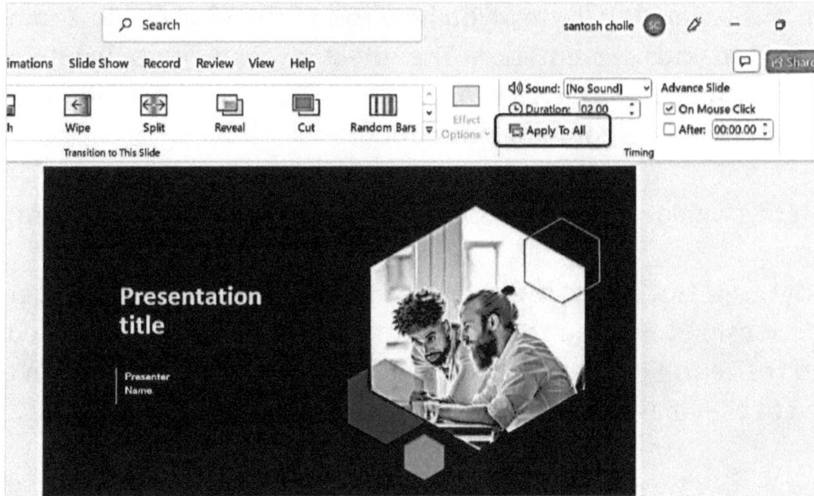

The transition and timing that you have set will be automatically applied to all the slides in your presentation.

Let's explore the Morph transition, which is one of the newest slide transitions available in PowerPoint. The Morph transition works differently from the other transitions, and you can learn more about it in my Morph and Zoom in PowerPoint post.

That's all for slide transitions. Use them to add a visually appealing effect to your next presentation.

The Morph Option & Zoom in PowerPoint

If you haven't yet explored the new Morph function in PowerPoint, you're in for a treat. It's a fun new feature to demonstrate during PowerPoint training.

In this segment, I'll show you how to use the Morph and Zoom effect in your presentation. The effect involves zooming into a specific area of your screen and then zooming out to another location before zooming back out.

Here's a guide on how to use the Morph feature in PowerPoint:

My top tip is to use high-resolution images with larger dimensions. For the zoom effect to work correctly, we'll need to resize the images, and high resolution is crucial if you don't want the images to appear blurry or pixelated.

Let's start by creating a new blank presentation:

- Launch Microsoft PowerPoint.

The PowerPoint Edge - Mastering the Art of Storytelling

- Create a new blank presentation.

- Change the slide layout to "Blank."

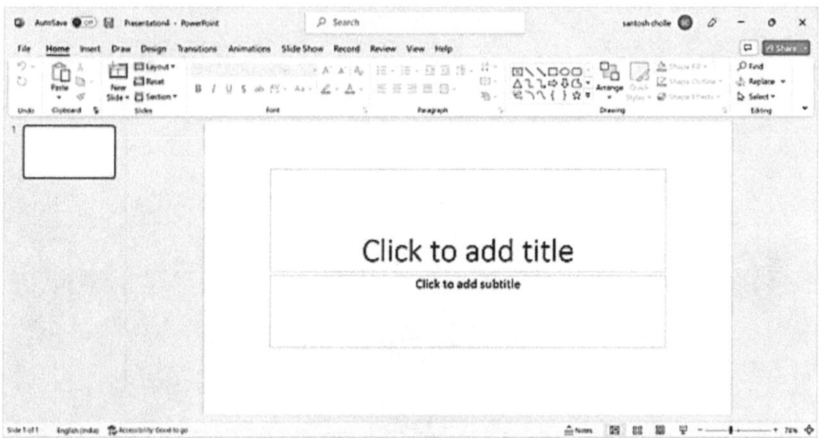

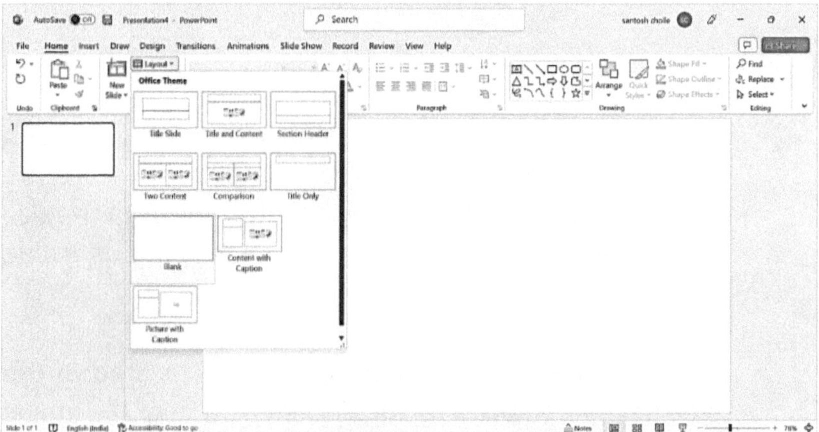

- Next, we have to add the picture we want to use on the slide.

- Go to the Insert tab and click on Pictures > This Device

- Browse and select a picture on your computer that you want to use, and then click on Open

- The picture will now be inserted into the slide.

- To make sure that the entire slide area is covered with the picture, I will resize it. Keep in mind that since the dimensions of the image may be different from the size of the slide, some parts of the picture may not be visible on the slide.

- Use the thumbnail version of the slide located in the side navigation pane to adjust the position of the image so that the desired parts are visible.

- After setting up the first slide, we need to create a duplicate of it.

- To do this, right-click on the slide in the navigation pane and select "Duplicate Slide," or select the slide with your mouse and press "Ctrl + D" on your keyboard.

- For the second slide, you will need to resize the image to display only the section you want to show when zoomed in. To do this, zoom out to 33% and adjust the image size to 50cm wide. You can see in the thumbnail on the left that only a portion of the original image is showing, and I have outlined the slide area to show how much of the image is displayed on that slide.

- To create another slide with a different part of the image, duplicate slide 1 once more and resize the image again to show a different section.

- Move this duplicate slide to the end of the presentation (slide 3).

- Resize the image again and position it to show the second point you want to morph to.

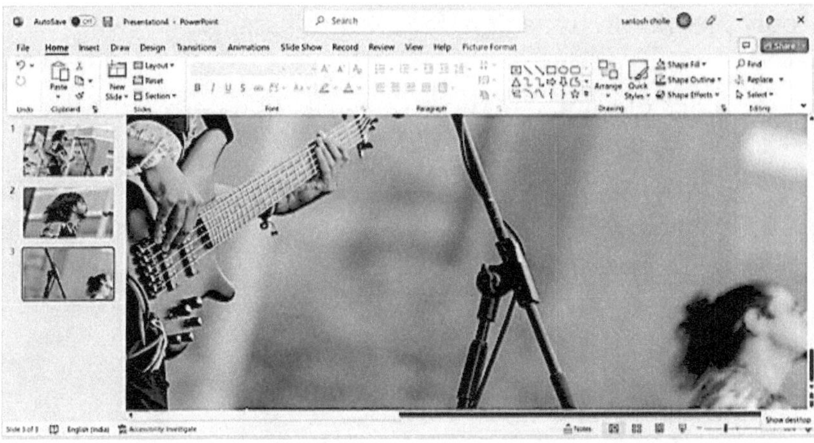

- To complete the morph and zoom effect, duplicate slide 1 one more time and place it at the end of the slide deck. This will serve as the final slide that zooms back out to show the original full image again.

- By now, you should have a total of 4 slides in your presentation.

Apply the morph transition, follow these steps:

- Click on slide 2 in the slide navigation pane.

- Hold down the Ctrl key on your keyboard and select slide 3 and 4.

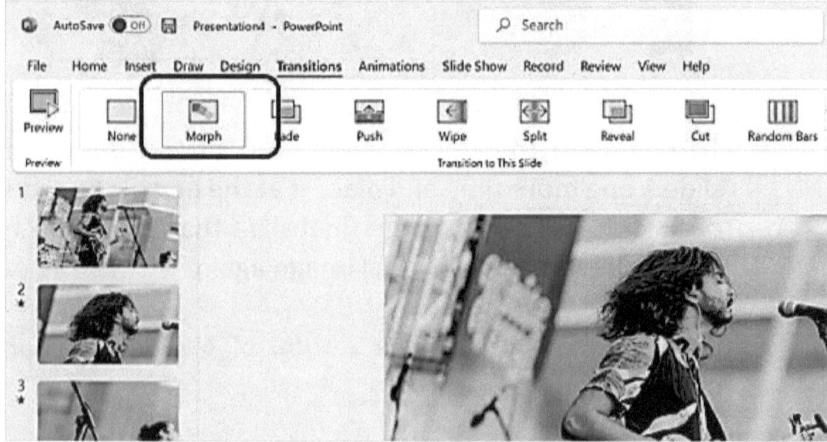

A star icon will appear under the slide numbers 2, 3, and 4 in the navigation pane, indicating that the Morph transition has been applied to these slides. No need to apply the Morph transition to the first slide.

Run the slide show:

Now, we need to automate the slide show so that it progresses through the slides without requiring manual clicks or keyboard presses. By default, you have to click the mouse or press a key on the keyboard to move from one slide to the next. To automate this process, follow these steps:

Ensure you are still on the Transitions tab.

- Uncheck the "On Mouse Click" option.

- Check the box for "After" and set the duration for each slide to show, such as 2 seconds.

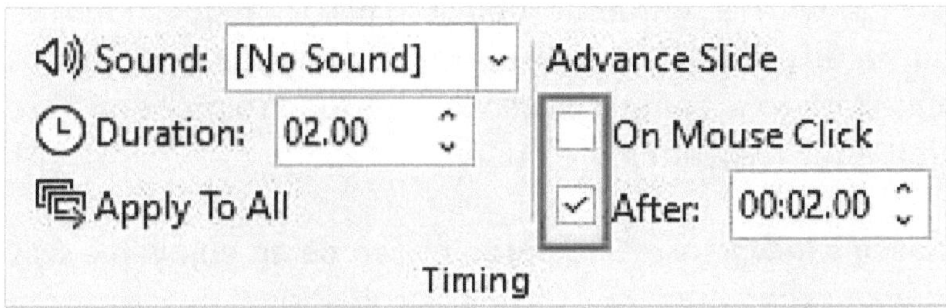

- Repeat the aforementioned steps for each of Slide 2, 3 and 4. (Note that if you select the 'Apply to All' button, the timing options will be applied to all the slides, but the morph transition will be removed from Slide 2, 3 and 4, and you would need to reapply the transition to each slide.)

- To begin the slide show, press the F5 key on the keyboard.

- The presentation should commence, and after the predetermined timing, the slide will morph and zoom to the initial location of the image, and then continue along the slide deck. I trust that this has provided you with an entertaining introduction to the Morph and Zoom feature. Keep an eye out for more posts on Morph in PowerPoint.

Create an animation in PowerPoint to show and hide an object.

Recently, I came across an intriguing query on an online forum about Microsoft PowerPoint. The user wanted to know how to display an object on the screen for a brief period and then replace it with a different object. This is a question I've encountered several times during my training sessions, and it's a simple task to accomplish. Hence, I decided to mention here about it after answering the query.

Animations in Microsoft PowerPoint can be an enjoyable way to let your creativity flow. Through professional development programs for teachers, I have discovered several innovative ways that PowerPoint and animations, in particular, can be leveraged in classrooms by teachers and students alike.

About Animations.

Rewritten: Animations in Microsoft PowerPoint are an excellent way to make presentations more interactive and dynamic. There are four types of animations available, namely Entrance, Emphasis, Exit, and Motion Paths, and the choice of animation depends on what the object needs to do. If an object needs to appear or disappear, an Entrance or Exit effect is used. If it needs to be highlighted or accentuated, an Emphasis effect is used. Motion Paths effects offer great flexibility to create custom paths, including loops and turns. However, excessive use of animations can be overwhelming and distracting for the audience. While animations can improve information retention, it is best to use them sparingly to avoid confusion.

About Animation Pane.

The Animation Pane is a tool in Microsoft PowerPoint that lets you see all objects on a slide that have animation effects applied to them. By using the Animation Pane, you can get a clearer view of which objects are animated and when their animations will start. This feature is also helpful in diagnosing and fixing issues related to animations. Note that the Animation Pane is hidden by default and can be accessed by clicking on a specific button, which I will explain later in this post.

Lest begin with Animations.

Starting now, we will work on an animation sequence in which an image of a Frog transforms into a beautiful Prince. This idea came from on old story on 'The Prince Who Turns into a Frog'.

To achieve this, we will use animations in PowerPoint. Here's how to get started:

- Open Microsoft PowerPoint.

- Choosing the correct slide layout is crucial, so for this animation sequence, we need a blank slide. Click on the "Home" tab and then on the "Layout" button, and choose "Blank" from the available options.

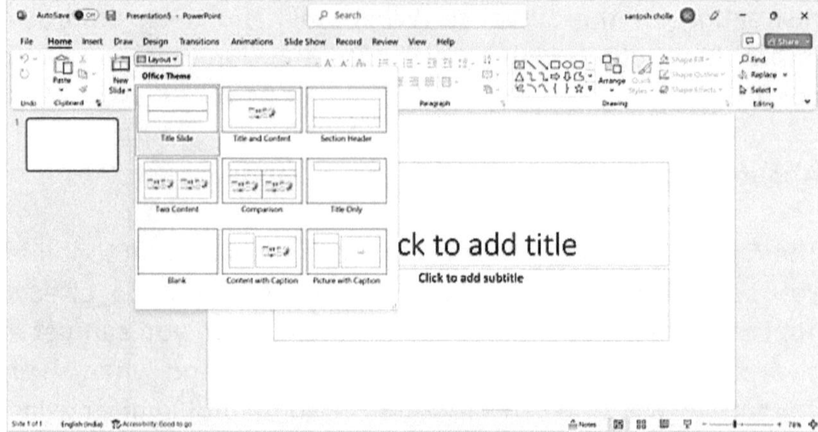

- To add the initial image, navigate to the Insert tab and select Pictures.

- This will bring up the Insert Picture dialogue box.

- Our next step is to add the first image, which will be of a Frog.

- If you require images for your presentation, you can use the built-in "Insert" > "Online Pictures" tool. However, be sure to verify copyright requirements on the chosen image. Alternatively, you can perform a Google search and filter images labelled for reuse, or use a stock image library like Pexels.com.

- To add the Frog image, navigate to the "Insert" tab and select "Pictures."

- This action will open the "Insert Picture" dialog box.

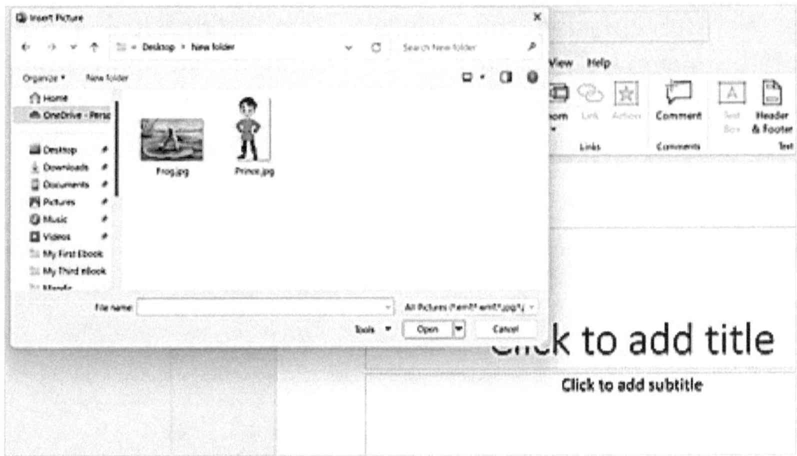

- Select the first image and click Insert

- The Frog is now displayed on the slide:

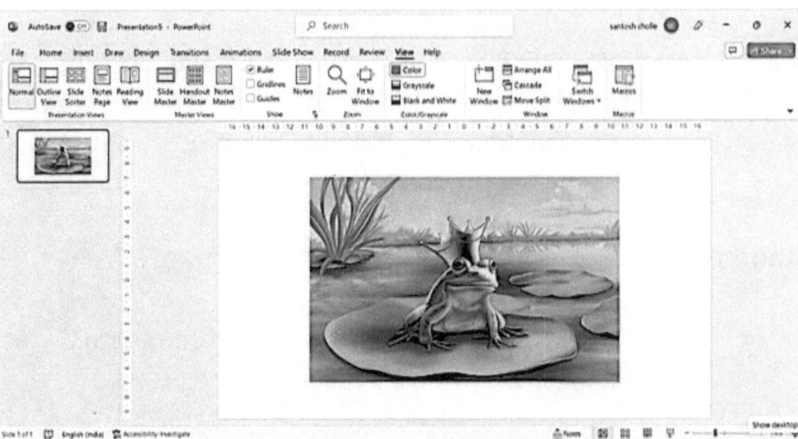

- In order to incorporate the Prince, replicate the procedure employed for the initial image.

- After placing the Prince on the slide, it may be necessary to adjust its dimensions to an appropriate size. Subsequently, relocate the Prince to one side of the slide by clicking and dragging the image.

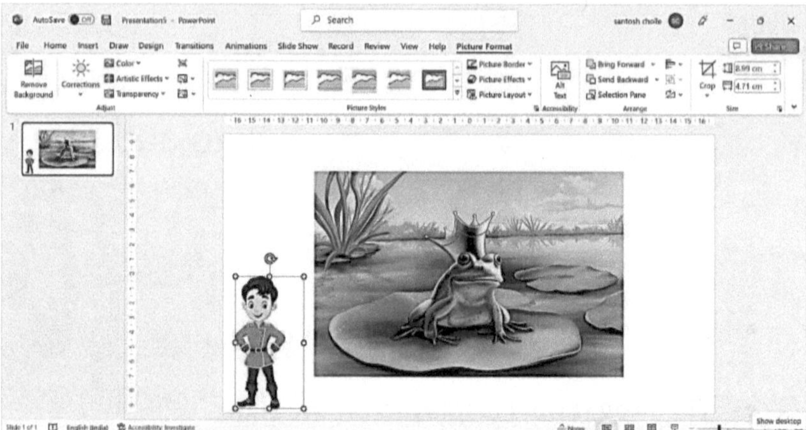

- I recommend shifting the Prince to a side currently to simplify the process of configuring the animation sequence. Towards the end, we will relocate the Prince above the Frog and enlarge it.

Animation.

- Opt for the Frog and access the "Animations" tab situated on the Ribbon by clicking it.

- In order to exhibit the Animation Pane, click the "Animation Pane" button that can be found in the "Advanced Animation" category.

- Subsequently, the Animation Pane will materialize on the right-hand side of the slide.

- Our objective for the Frog is to make it vanish.

- Choose the "More" button located underneath the downward scrolling arrow in the Animation gallery.

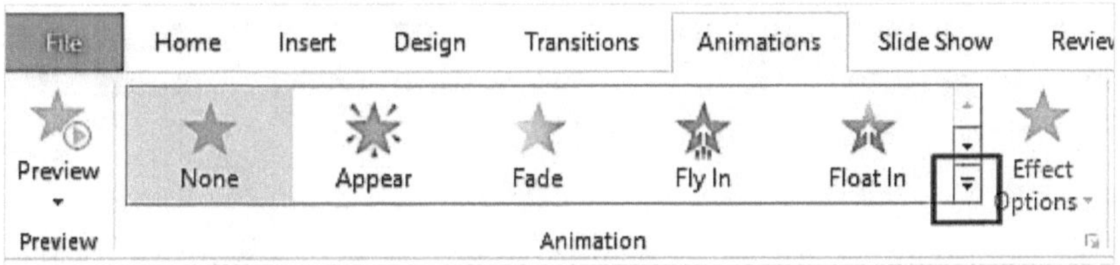

- Navigate through the available animations list and locate the "Exit" category, then opt for the "Disappear" animation type.

- Upon doing so, a square with the number 1 will materialize on the top left corner of the image.

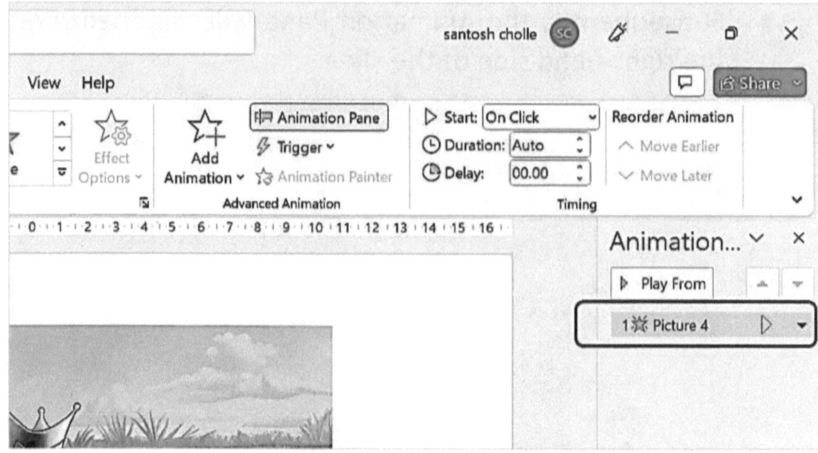

The square number aids in identifying objects in a sequence, indicating that this particular animation will be executed as the first item in the sequence. It's worth noting that if multiple animations are set to run simultaneously, they will all be assigned the same number instead of individual numbers.

Timing:

The majority of animations are dependent on timing, which entails specifying when an animation will commence, its duration, and whether any delay is required.

Regarding the "Start" option, there are three alternatives available:

On Click

To commence the animation sequence while in slideshow mode, either click the mouse or press any key.

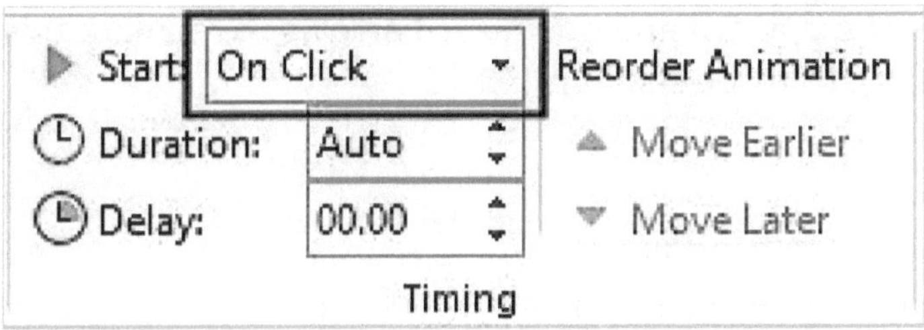

After Previous

The animation sequence will initiate once all preceding animation effects have finished. Note that the start of a slideshow also qualifies as a "preceding" effect.

With Previous

The animation sequence will start simultaneously with any preceding animation effects, including the commencement of a slideshow, which is also considered a "preceding" effect.

During training, a question that often arises at this stage is, "Why are we using After Previous when this is the first item in the sequence?" This is a legitimate inquiry, and as explained in the table above, PowerPoint acknowledges that when we begin a presentation in slideshow mode, it qualifies as the "previous" effect, and therefore an animation will commence automatically without requiring any clicks.

- Regarding the "Duration" option, we must specify the time it will take for the animation to complete. In this case, we need to determine how long until our Frog vanishes.

- Use the upward and downward arrows to regulate this setting to three seconds (03.00).

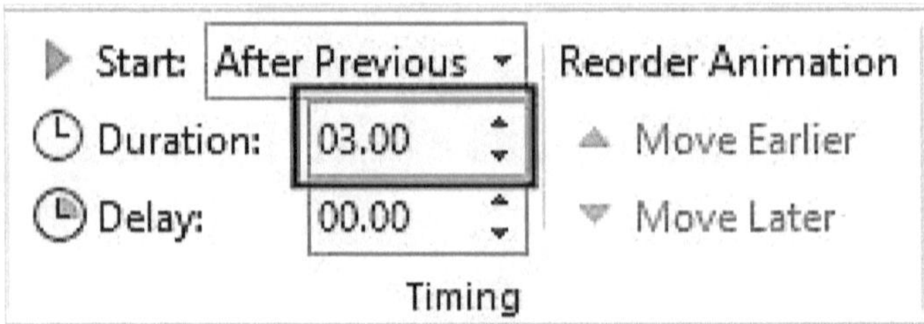

- We won't be using a delay for this sequence.

- Choose the Prince image.

- In the Animation gallery, select the Appear option from the More button.

- In the Timing section, change the Start setting to After Previous since we want the Prince to appear once the Frog has vanished.

- We can leave the Duration setting as the default option of Auto for now. This means the Prince will remain on the slide until we move to another slide or exit the slideshow. If you intend to include a third or fourth animation, specify the number of seconds you want the Prince to appear.

- The images are now animated. Click and drag the Prince over the Frog and increase the image size.

The PowerPoint Edge - Mastering the Art of Storytelling

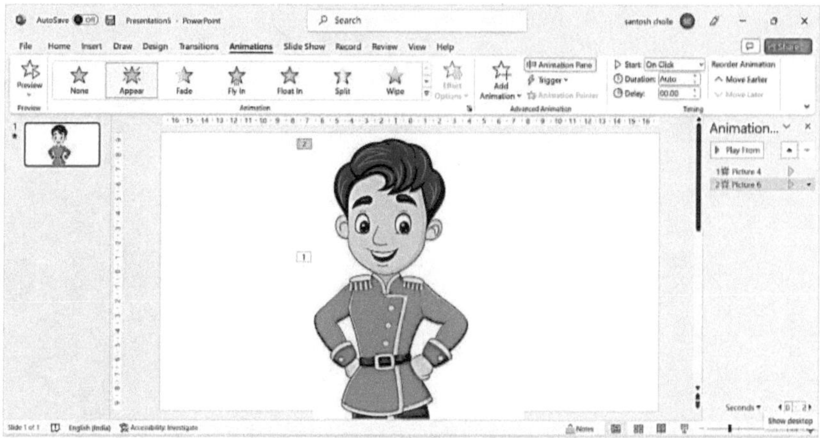

- The animation is now ready to be previewed.

- Select the first object in the Animation Pane, which is the Frog in our case.

- Click on the Preview button from the Animations ribbon.

- A preview of the animation will now appear.

- To view the complete animation in slideshow mode, press F5 on your keyboard and enjoy the show.

- After the animation has ended, hit Esc on your keyboard to exit.

- Congratulations! You have successfully created a simple yet effective animation in PowerPoint. I encourage you to explore the vast range of animation possibilities that PowerPoint offers.

13

Inbuilt templates in PowerPoint presentations

The PowerPoint Edge - Mastering the Art of Storytelling

The PowerPoint Edge - Mastering the Art of Storytelling

Have you ever wanted to create a PowerPoint presentation quickly without spending too much time on design, colours, and slide layouts? Well, there's a simple solution. You can use the built-in templates available through the Microsoft Office template gallery to create an effective PowerPoint presentation in no time.

The Microsoft Office template gallery offers a range of pre-designed templates for PowerPoint presentations that include formatting for various aspects of the presentation, such as background patterns, fonts, colours, and overall design. Instead of starting from scratch, these templates can save you time and effort. They cater to specific audiences and design styles, with options ranging from modern presentations to those suitable for high schoolers or architecture-based slideshows. Spending just 10 minutes exploring the templates can be worthwhile while enjoying a cup of coffee or tea.

A piece of advice that I often give to participants in my training courses is to be curious and explorative. It's important to remember that there may be features or resources available that you are not aware of. Therefore, take the time to navigate around the program and discover new options and tools.

There are individuals who express their dislike towards template options, stating that they are too common and should be avoided. However, my personal opinion is that any feature within the Office suite that can save time is valuable, including templates. If a template can save me several hours of design work, I am more than willing to use it.

Let's now dive into the process of using a template to create a new PowerPoint presentation without any delay.

How to use a pre-designed template to create a PowerPoint presentation

- Open Microsoft PowerPoint

- Choose "New" by clicking on the "File" tab.

- The pre-installed templates will now appear:

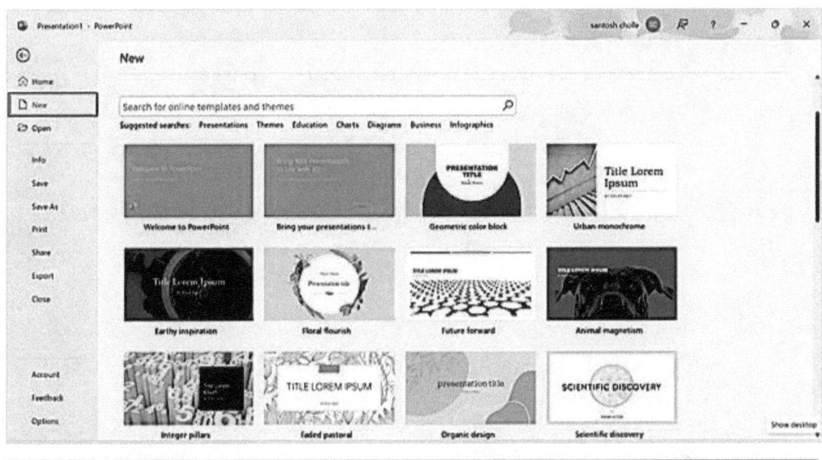

- At the top of the screen, there is a search box that enables you to search for keywords related to a specific topic or design style.

- Some suggested search terms are located below the search bar.

- It's advisable to spend 10-15 minutes browsing through the various categories to explore the available options. This way, you can discover what you might utilize.

- To find business-related presentations, select "Business" from the suggested search terms and browse through the options.

- Single-click on a design you wish to use, and a preview will appear.

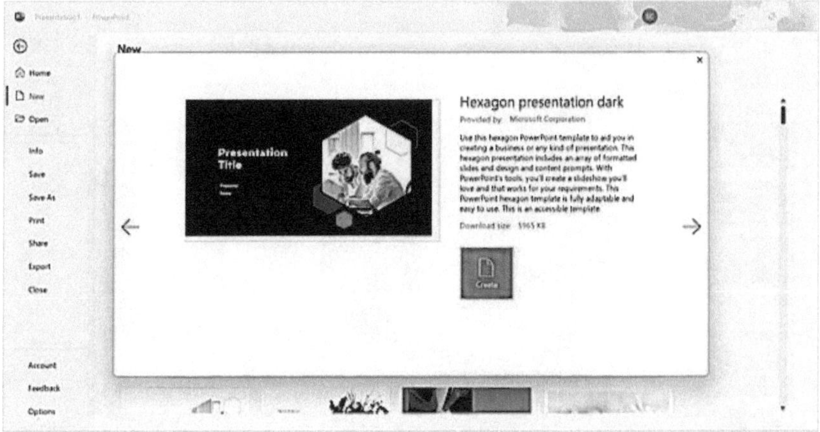

- To use the selected template, click on the "Create" button. If you want to browse further and select a different template, click on the "X" button and continue exploring until you find the right one.

- After clicking on "Create," the template will be downloaded from the Office.com website and displayed in PowerPoint.

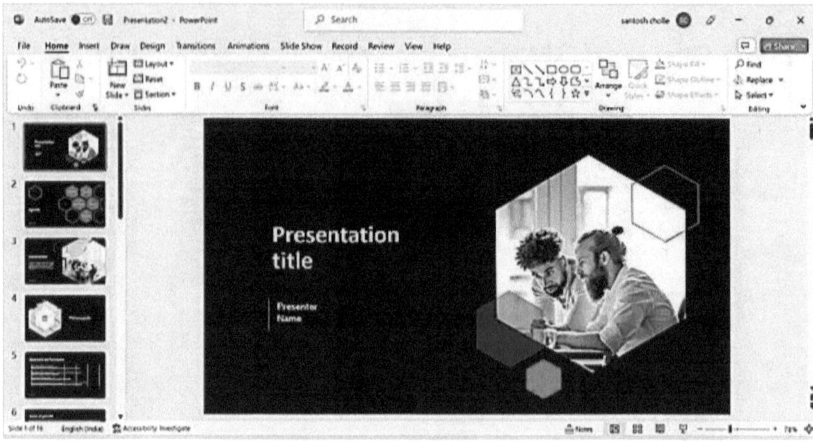

- You can now take some time to explore the various slide layouts and design elements like images, SmartArt graphics, charts, and tables included in the template.

How to add speaker notes in PowerPoint

In order to give an effective presentation, it's important to have a clear understanding of the topic and be able to deliver the content in a coherent manner. However, it can be challenging to remember everything that needs to be said, especially if multiple presenters are involved. This is where speaker notes come in handy. Speaker notes can serve as reminders of what needs to be discussed on each slide and can be particularly useful for new presenters or those sharing the presentation with others.

In this guide, we'll go through the process of adding speaker notes to each slide in your PowerPoint presentation. This will allow you to use the Presenter View feature in PowerPoint to deliver your presentation with confidence.

To add speaker notes to individual slides, follow these steps:

- Open Microsoft PowerPoint.

- Select "Open Other Presentation" from the Start screen, or choose a presentation from the Recent list.

- Make sure that Slide 1 is currently displayed, which is usually the opening title slide.

- If the Notes area is not displayed underneath the slide, click the Notes button located in the Status bar.

- Click on the "Click to add notes" area at the bottom of the screen where you want to add the speaker notes.

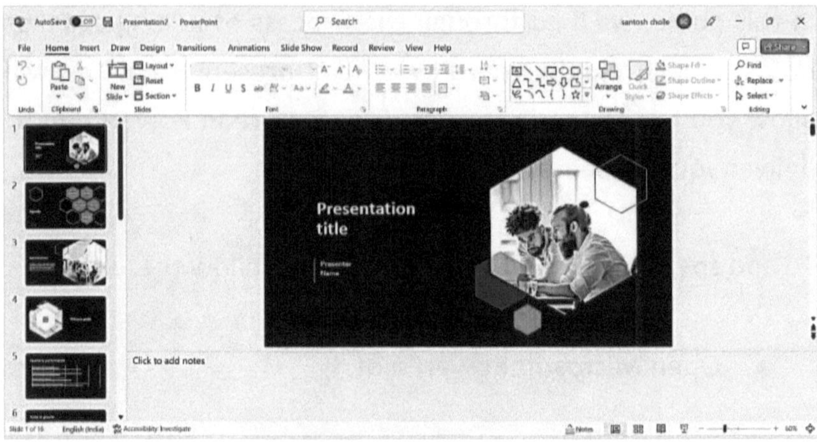

Are you creating a presentation and need to keep track of what to say on each slide? One way to do this is by adding speaker notes to your PowerPoint presentation. Speaker notes can provide you with a quick reference to what needs to be discussed on each slide and help you deliver your presentation with ease.

To add speaker notes to your presentation, follow these steps:

- Open Microsoft PowerPoint.

- Open the presentation you want to add speaker notes to.

- Click on the slide you want to add notes to.

- If the Notes pane is not visible, click the Notes button located in the status bar.

- Click in the Notes pane and enter your notes for the slide.

- Keep your notes brief and use bullet points or key information you want to discuss.

- Use font formatting options to make your notes easier to read.

- Repeat the process for all slides in your presentation.

To view your speaker notes, follow these steps:

- Click on the View tab.

- Click on Notes Page.

- The Notes Page view will display a snapshot of the slide and show the corresponding notes at the bottom of the page.

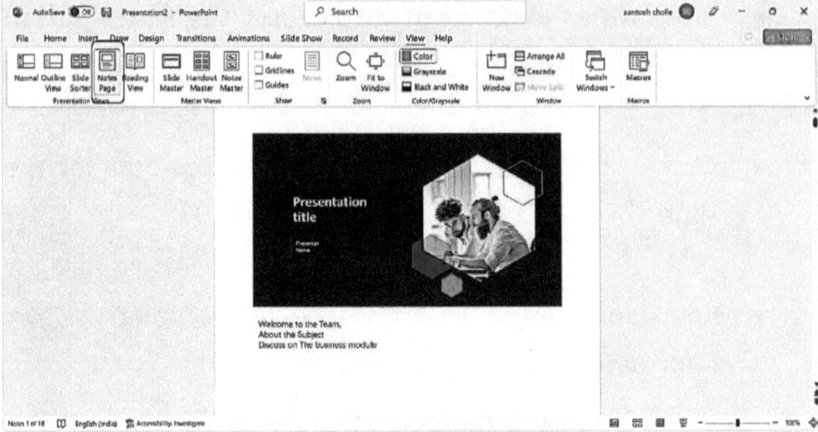

- Navigate between each slide using the up and down scroll bar.

- Return to the normal view by selecting View > Normal.

Displaying speaker notes during a presentation

Presenter view is a feature in Microsoft PowerPoint that allows you to view your speaker notes while projecting the slides for your audience. This can help guide you through the presentation while keeping the audience focused on the content.

Presenter view works on operating systems that support multiple displays, such as Microsoft Windows 7 or higher. To use Presenter view, you need a computer with multiple monitor capability. If you are unsure whether your computer has this capability, check with the manufacturer.

For users of Microsoft PowerPoint 2013 or PowerPoint 2016, connecting a monitor or data projector will automatically set up Presenter view. If you are using a computer with a single monitor, you can still use Presenter view, but it's recommended to test it beforehand to avoid technical issues during your live presentation.

To enable Presenter view, follow these steps:

- Select Slide Show > Set Up Slide Show.

- Under the Multiple monitors section, select the checkbox for Use Presenter View.

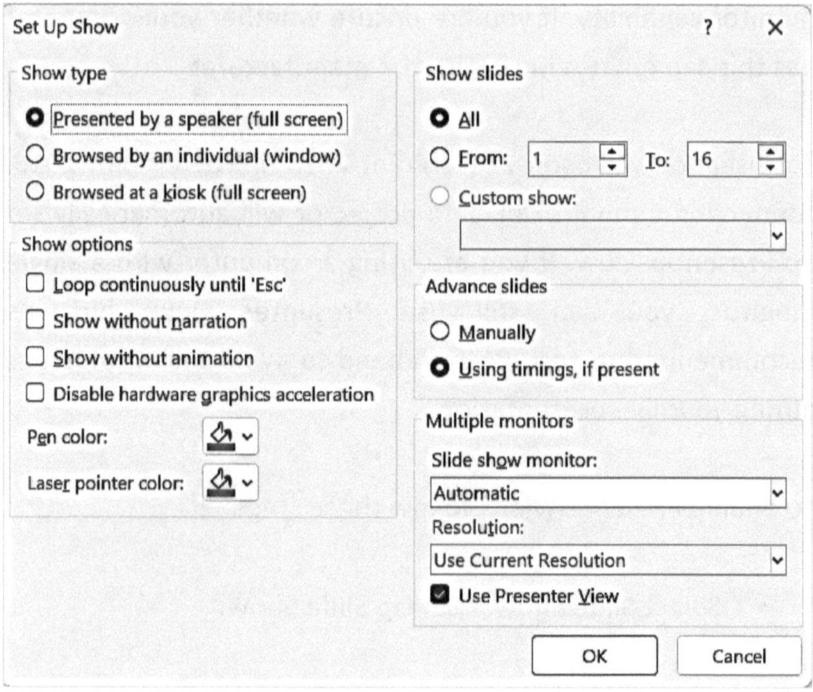

- Click the "OK" button to save your settings.

- Press the "F5" key to start the slide show in Presenter View.

- Now, Microsoft PowerPoint will display your slide show in Presenter View.

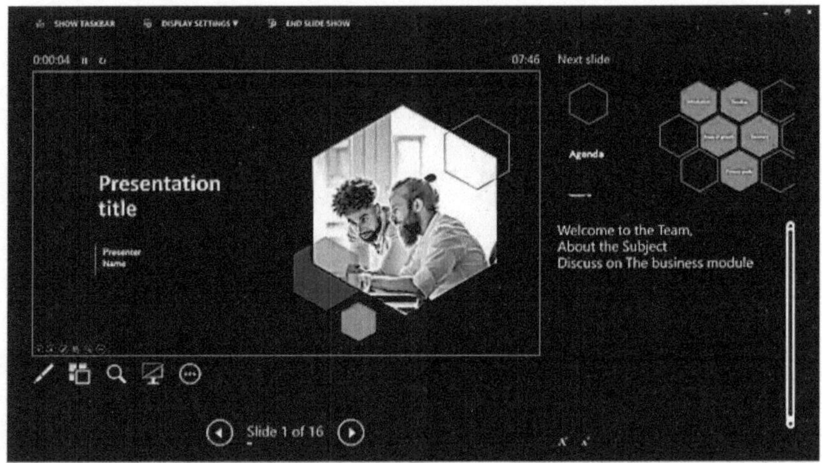

If you have connected a data projector to your computer, Presenter View will be automatically displayed on your computer screen.

However, if you are using PowerPoint on a computer with a single monitor, you can still use Presenter View by launching your presentation and clicking on the More button. Then, choose the option Show Presenter View.

Congratulations on successfully adding speaker notes and enabling Presenter View for your presentation.

14

Rehearse timings of your PowerPoint presentation

A common worry for presenters is finding the right amount of content for their presentation. The Rehearse Timings feature in Microsoft PowerPoint offers an easy and efficient way to practice the timing of your presentation. This feature helps you determine if you need to add more detail or remove some content. In my experience, I have always had a specific timeframe for my presentations. I want to avoid having too much content that would make me rush through the material, but I also don't want to finish too quickly.

It is important to note that the rehearsed timings are only a guide. They help you rehearse the time it will take to present your content from start to finish without any pauses. At the end of the rehearsal, you can choose to save the timings to your presentation, which will automate the transition between slides. However, I personally prefer to advance the slides manually as it allows me to answer questions or provide additional information on a topic prompted by the audience.

Let's get started

If you want to use rehearse timings in PowerPoint, here are the steps you need to follow:

- Launch Microsoft PowerPoint

- Open the presentation that you want to rehearse timings for, or create a new Blank Presentation and add some sample content.

- Click on the "Slide Show" tab in the ribbon.

- Select "Rehearse Timings" option from the "Set Up" group.

- The Rehearsal toolbar will appear, and the presentation will start in Slide Show mode.

The Rehearsal toolbar will start timing your presentation, so you can begin rehearsing it.

- Practice your presentation script for Slide 1.

- After you finish talking about Slide 1, wait for a few extra seconds and then click the "Next" button on the "Rehearsal" toolbar.

- You will now see Slide 2, where you can present the content related to it.

- Keep repeating this process for all the slides, using the "Next" button to move to the next slide. In case you need to pause for a moment, click the "Pause" button on the Rehearsal toolbar.

- After you finish the entire presentation, a prompt will appear asking if you want to save the slide timings.

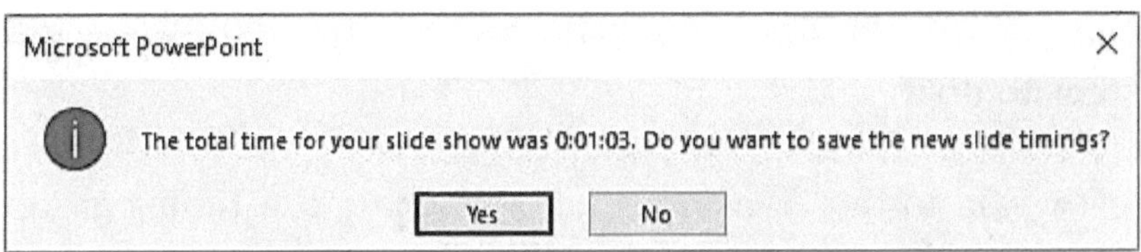

- To utilize the saved timings and enable automatic slide advancement during your presentation, click "Yes."

- If you choose not to use the saved timings, take note of the total presentation time and click "No."

- If you saved the slide timings, navigate to the Transitions tab and verify that the Advanced Slide After setting is enabled. The rehearsed timing duration will now be applied to each slide.

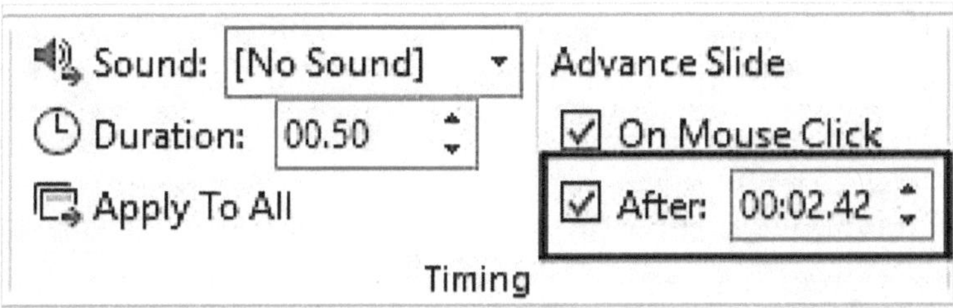

To check the rehearsed timings, click on "Slide Show" and then select "From Beginning," or press the F5 key on your keyboard.

Manually set Advance Slide

If you want to manually set the timing for each slide transition, you can use the "Advance Slide After" setting. Here are the steps to do it:

- Go to the Transitions tab and locate the Timing group on the right side of the Ribbon.

- The "After" option will already be enabled, displaying the duration set in the Rehearse Timings feature.

- You can manually adjust the amount of time that PowerPoint will wait before automatically advancing the slide.

- Edit the After setting for each slide, displayed in minutes and seconds with two decimal places (e.g., 00:02.50 for 2.5 seconds).

- If you want to apply the same setting for all slides, specify the time period and click the "Apply to All" button.

Note that when you apply an advance slide option to all slides, any transition effect settings you have set will also be applied to all other slides.

To manually advance the slides during your presentation, follow these steps:

- Go to the Transitions tab in the Ribbon.

- In the Timing group, deselect the "After" option and leave only the "On Mouse Click" checkbox enabled.

- Click "Apply to All."

To test your presentation, press F5 on the keyboard. Your slides will advance only when you click the mouse or press the space bar on the keyboard.

If you prefer to advance the slides yourself during your presentation, you can use this method to have greater flexibility to engage with your audience and answer their questions.

I hope these tips have been helpful, and remember to have fun and enjoy your time presenting!

15

Embed a YouTube video in a PowerPoint slide

To most online sources, Microsoft PowerPoint has been around since circa 1990, and it continues to age gracefully. Gone are the days of sitting through monotonous presentations, as modern presentations have become more engaging and dynamic with the use of various types of media, such as video and animations. Incorporating such media can provide additional information and enhance the content, resulting in an audience that is attentive rather than bored.

Online video sources, such as YouTube and Vimeo, are a great way to add media content to presentations. While you can insert your own video, this can increase the file size of the presentation. However, by using content stored online, you can help keep your file sizes small. If you prefer to use your own video content but are concerned about file size, you can upload your content to YouTube and embed it back into PowerPoint.

There are two methods to include online video in your Microsoft PowerPoint presentation, and both require an active internet connection at the time of viewing the presentation. This is because you are linking to the video on the YouTube website and not making a local copy of your own. One method involves embedding a video using the "embed" code, and the other method will be described below.

Embed a video using the "embed" code

- Go to YouTube and locate a video you wish to use within your presentation

- Locate the Share button

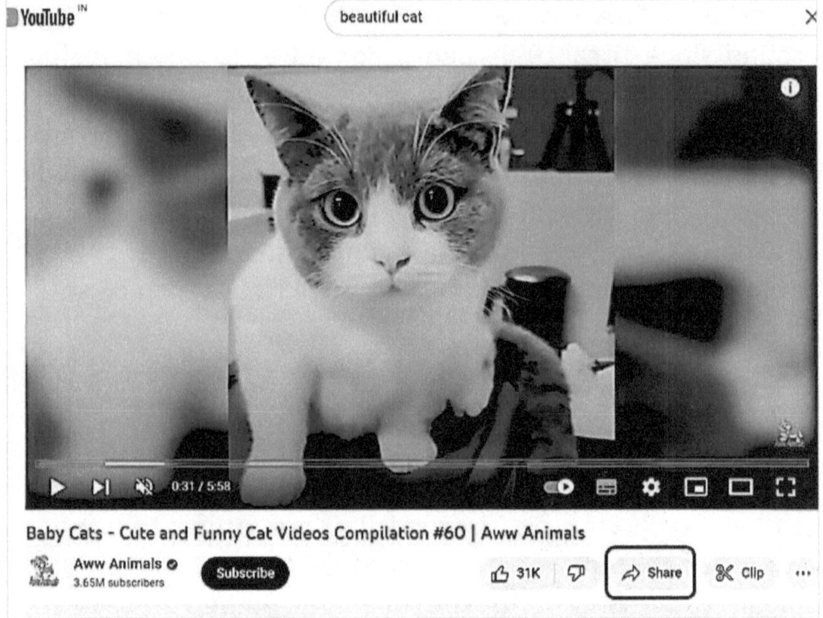

- Choose the "Embed" option from the sharing options.

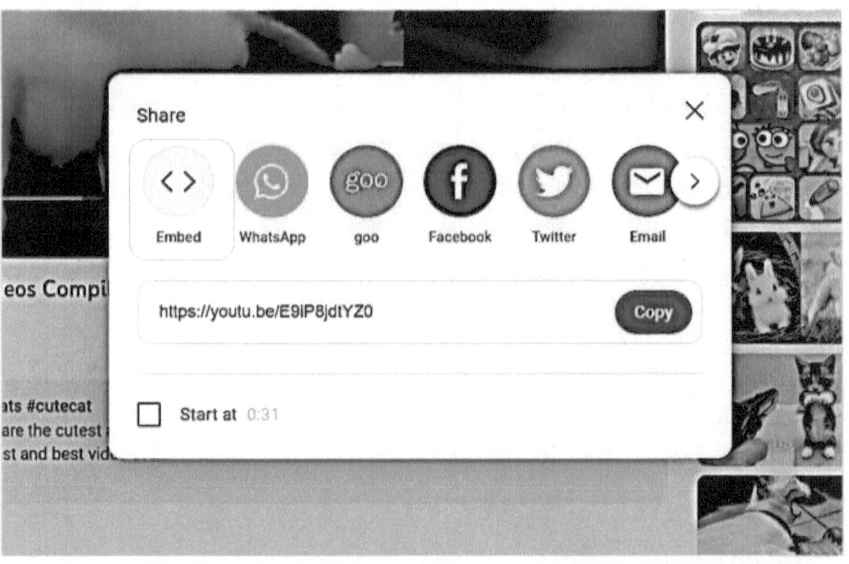

- The embed code should now start with "<iframe"...

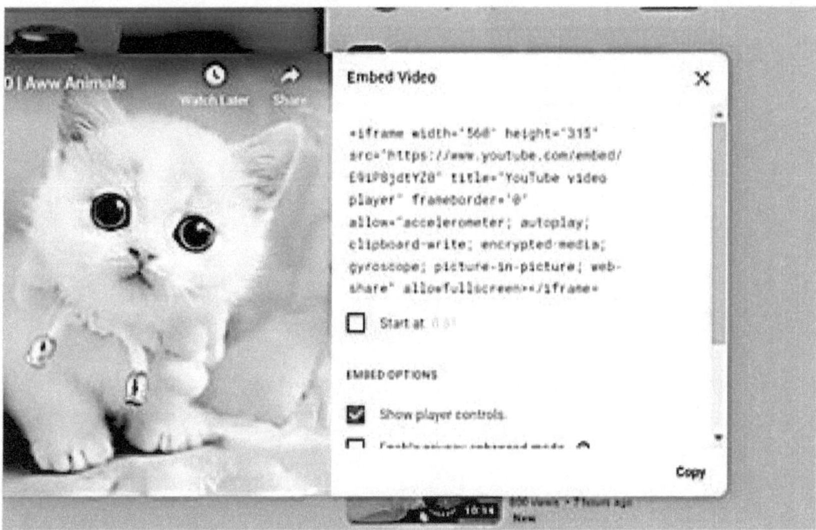

- Copy the code provided using the keyboard shortcut "Ctrl + C"

- Launch Microsoft PowerPoint and open the desired file to add the video or create a new presentation to experiment with.

- Click on "Insert" from the Ribbon menu and then choose "Video" followed by "Online Video."

The PowerPoint Edge - Mastering the Art of Storytelling

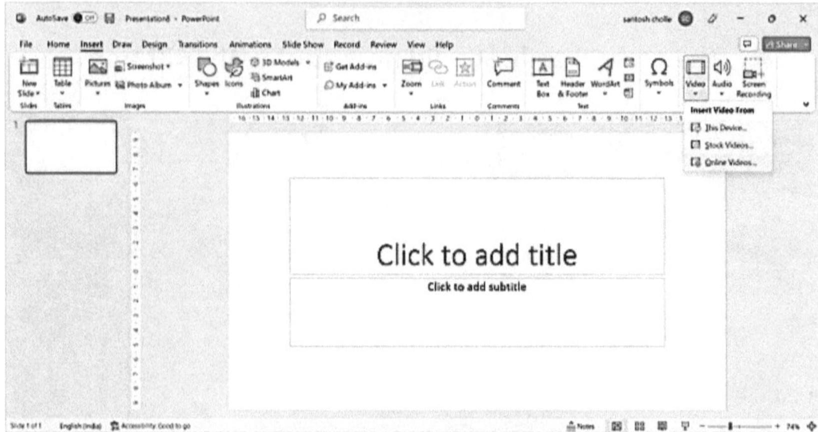

- You will see the Insert Video window:

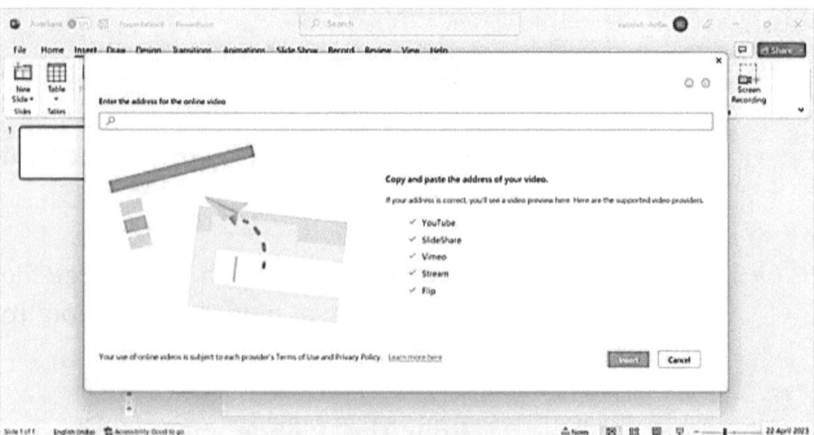

- Paste the embed code into the text box labelled "Enter the address of the online video" and press the Enter key.

- The video will be embedded into the slide.

- To preview the video, right-click on it and select "Preview," or click on "Play" in the Video Tools tab.

- You can adjust the size and position of the video like any other element on the slide.

To embed a video directly from YouTube:

- Open Microsoft PowerPoint and the file where you want to include the video or create a new blank presentation.

- Type in a keyword or phrase to search for the desired video in YouTube.

- A collection of videos matching your search criteria will be presented.

- Copy the link from the search bar of the browser.

- Past it under ' Enter the address for the online video.

- Click on 'Insert'

Hope These steps should make it easy for you to add a YouTube video to your Microsoft PowerPoint presentation.

16

Create a photo album slide show using PowerPoint

Have you ever been to an event where a slideshow of pictures was being displayed on a screen for everyone to see? Have you ever wondered how you could create one? Creating a slideshow using the Photo Album function in Microsoft PowerPoint is extremely simple.

I have personally utilized this feature to quickly put together photo albums for my pets' birthdays and other special occasions, and the response has always been positive. You can easily connect your computer to the latest television systems, allowing your photo album to be displayed on your LCD or digital TV. If you have access to a data projector, you could also connect your computer to it.

In addition to personal use, the photo album feature is also useful in a business setting, and can be used at demonstrations, trade shows, expos, or conferences. Why not use a photo album to document corporate events or the timeline of your project!

Create a photo album:

- Open Microsoft PowerPoint

- Ensure that a new, blank presentation is displayed

- Click on the Insert option from the Ribbon and then click on the Photo Album button.

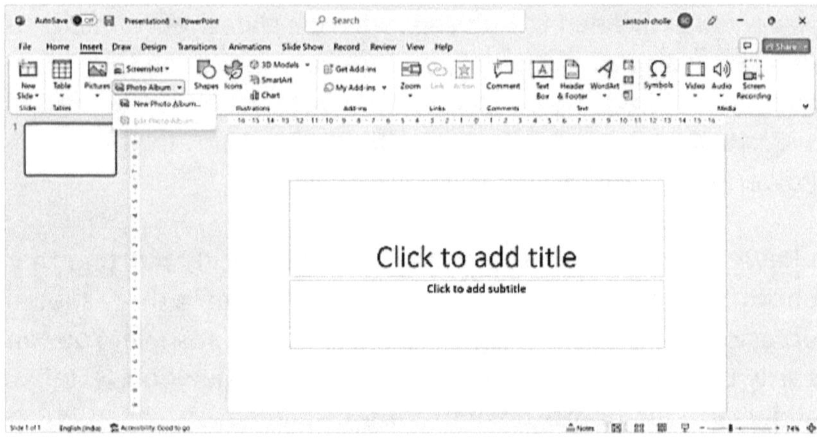

- The Photo Album dialog box will appear:

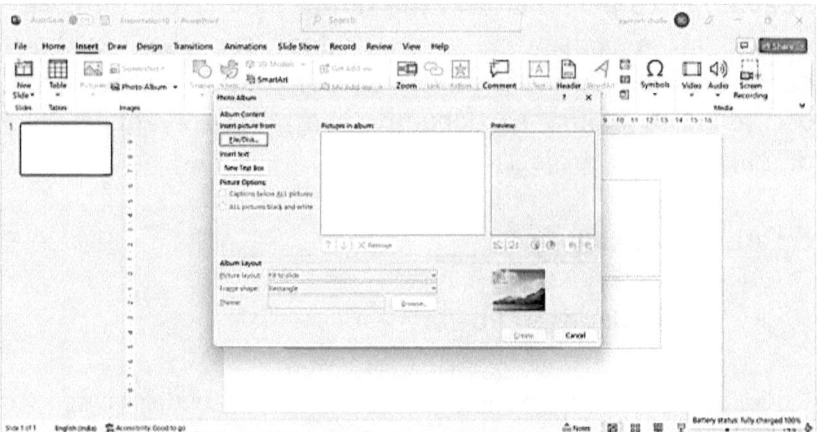

- To include pictures in your photo album, you must import them.

- Click on the File/Disk button to browse through your computer's hard drive.

- Find the pictures you want to import.

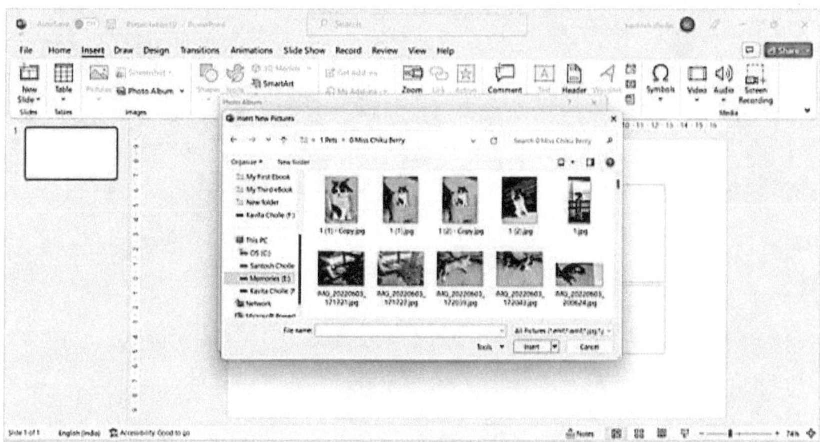

- It's alright if the pictures are in different locations; simply repeat the process for each location until all the desired pictures are imported.

- Next, you must choose the pictures to insert. Here's a helpful tip for saving time: don't import pictures individually. Instead, select several pictures at once by holding down the Ctrl key on your keyboard and clicking on them with the left mouse button.

- As a result, multiple file names will appear in the File name box.

The PowerPoint Edge - Mastering the Art of Storytelling

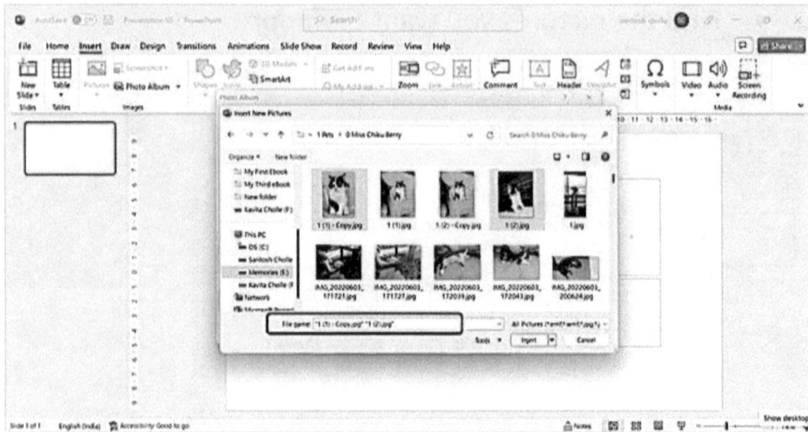

- After you have chosen the pictures from that location, click on Insert.

- Now, the pictures you selected will be listed in the Photo Album dialog box.

If you want to import more pictures, click on the File/Disk button once again and repeat the process.

Editing the Photos

One of the advantages of using the Photo Album feature is that it has built-in editing capabilities. While these are quite basic, they can save you time since you don't have to adjust your photos in another program before importing them into PowerPoint. You can easily flip a photo (which is helpful if a photo is displayed upside down), adjust the brightness and contrast of a photo, rearrange the order in which the photos are displayed, remove an accidentally imported photo, and even display all photos in black and white.

If you want to categorize your photos into different sections (e.g., displaying photos of your pet from birth to their current age), you can include a text box slide and insert text that indicates your pet's age.

- The first thing to do is to rearrange the order of your pictures.

- Tick the checkbox next to the first photo you want to move, and then use the up and down arrow buttons to position it in a new location in the list.

The PowerPoint Edge - Mastering the Art of Storytelling

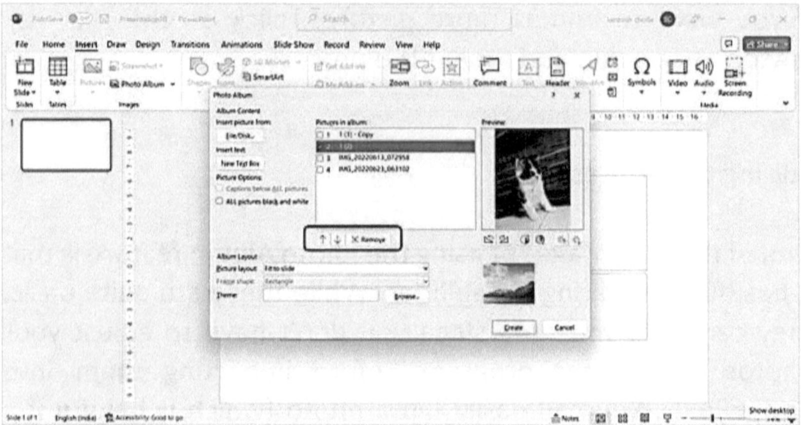

- I would like to add a text box to the beginning of my album and before the laptop photo.

- Click on the first picture and select "New Text Box."

- A new text box will now appear in the "Pictures in Album" list. You can type text into this box to display it in the photo album.

- To move this text box to the beginning of the album order, use the up arrow.

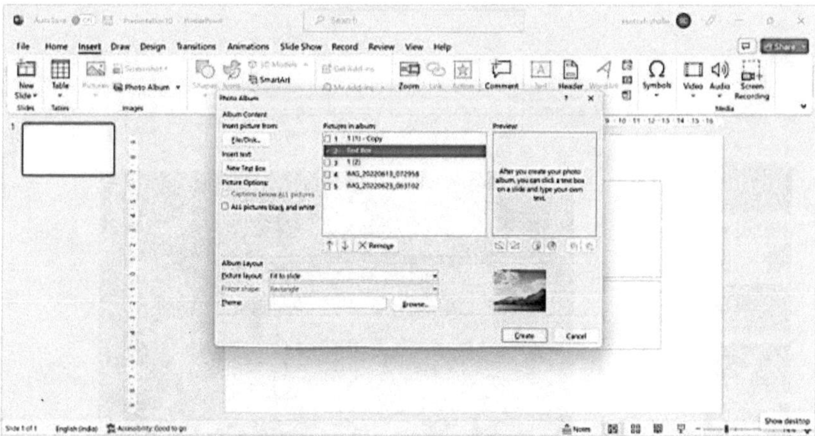

- Repeat this process to insert a new text box before another picture in your album.

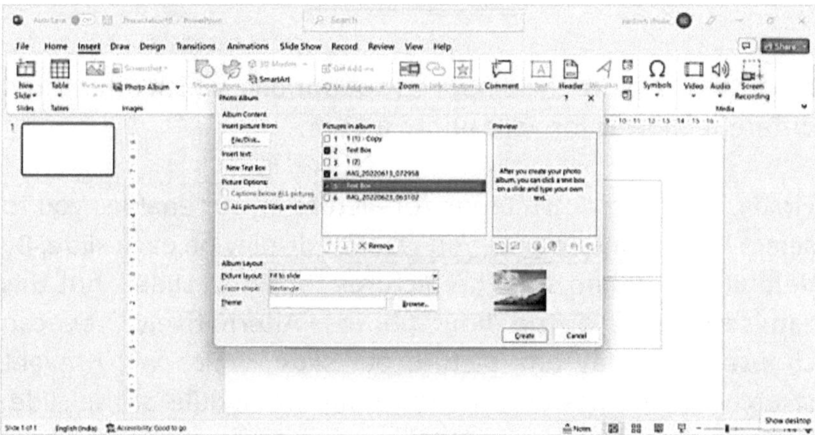

- Next, click on "Create" to preview the current state of our photo album.

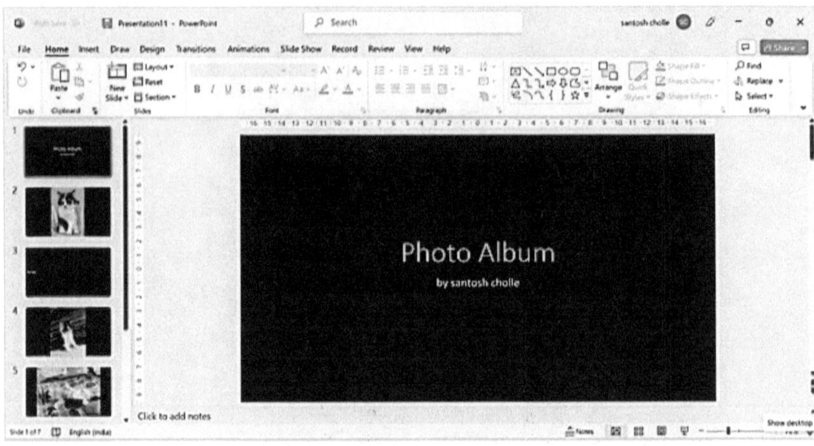

Album Layout

Next, we'll explore the album layout options, which offer three different choices for your photo album.

Firstly, the drop-down menu for Picture layout enables you to select how many pictures you want to display on each slide. By default, the album sets the pictures to "Fit to slide," but this can sometimes distort your photos. Alternatively, you can choose to display one picture per slide, which will prevent stretching, and position the photo in the middle of the slide. You can also display two, three, or up to four pictures on a single slide. Additionally, you have the option to include a title for each picture by selecting it from the Picture layout menu.

Secondly, the Frame shape drop-down menu lets you add stylish borders to your photos. You can opt for rounded corners, a simple frame, or even a darker frame.

Lastly, the Theme drop-down menu enables you to browse through the available design themes and select one to apply to your slides. The theme you choose will appear on the opening slide, any slides with a text box, and any slides where the picture isn't set to fit the entire slide.

Remember that you can modify these settings anytime to try out different layouts before choosing one that works best. Now that we've created the photo album and have the pictures on the slides, let's experiment with the layout.

- Go back to the Insert menu and click the arrow below the Photo Album button.

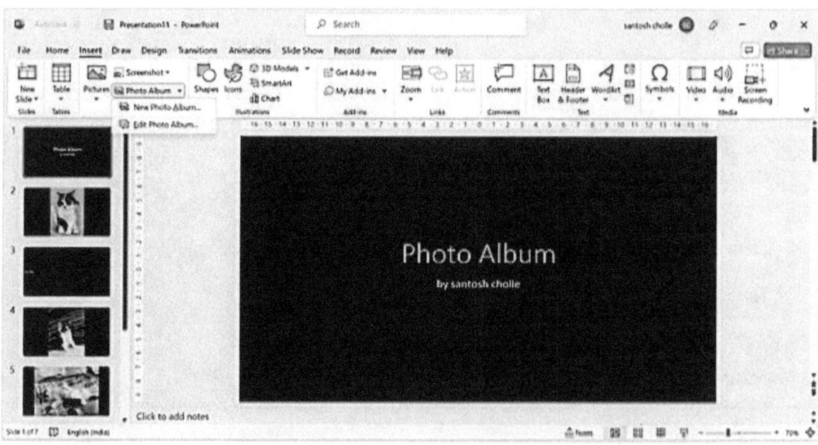

- Click on "Edit Photo Album" from the options located under the "Photo Album" button in the "Insert" menu.

- The "Edit Photo Album" dialog box will be displayed, which is identical to the previous dialog box.

- In the "Album Layout" section, select the "Picture layout" dropdown menu and choose "2 pictures".

- Change the "Frame shape" to "Rounded Rectangle".

- Click on "Update".

- The photo album will now be updated with 2 pictures on each slide, and you will notice that the previously inserted text boxes are included in the 2 pictures per slide layout.

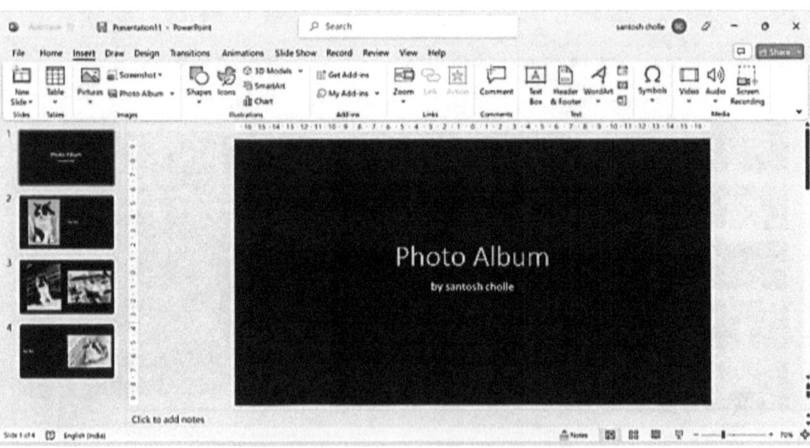

The PowerPoint Edge - Mastering the Art of Storytelling

- Navigate back to the Insert menu and select Photo Album, then click Edit Photo Album.

- If you want, you can continue to experiment with these settings, but if not, change the Picture layout back to Fit to slide.

- Next, let's apply a theme to our photo album.

- Click on the Browse button next to the Themes field.

- Note that the list of themes may appear as small icons, depending on which views you have set up for your folders in Microsoft Windows.

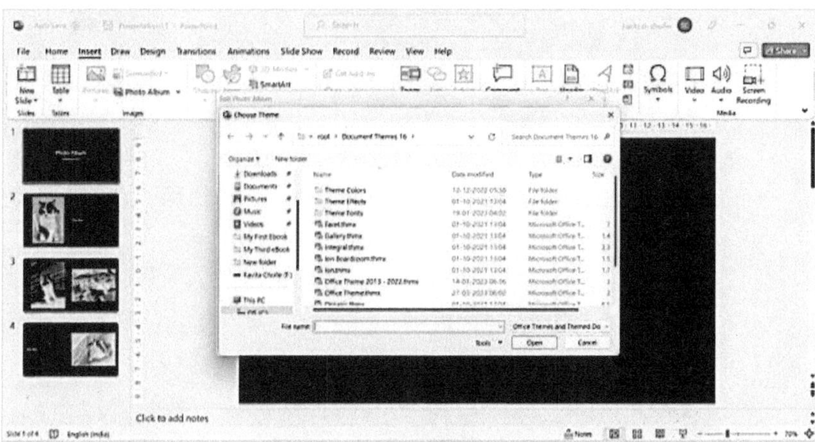

- The current view of the theme list can make it challenging to identify the preferred theme.

- To preview a theme, click on the "More options" arrow.

- Opt for either "Large icons" or "Extra Large Icons" to get a better view of the themes and their design and colour schemes.

- Once you've identified a theme you like, click on it to select it.

- After selecting the theme, click on "Update" to preview the changes made in the photo album.

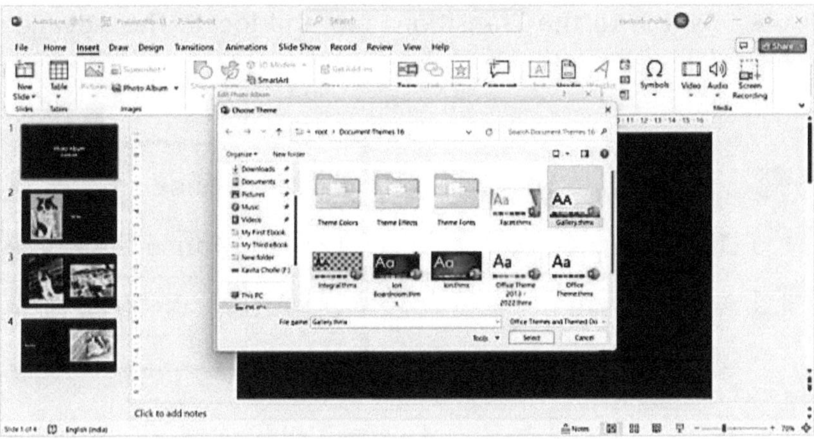

Finishing touches

To add the finishing touches to your photo album, such as titles and automatic playback, follow these steps:

Keep in mind that if you make changes to your photo album outside of the Photo Album dialog box and then update the photo album settings, you will lose those changes.

- Navigate to slide 1 which displays the title and author details of your photo album.

- Edit the text in the text boxes to display what you want.
- Repeat this step for any text boxes included in the photo album.

- To set up automatic playback at specific intervals:

- Switch to the Transitions tab and locate the Advance Slide controls.

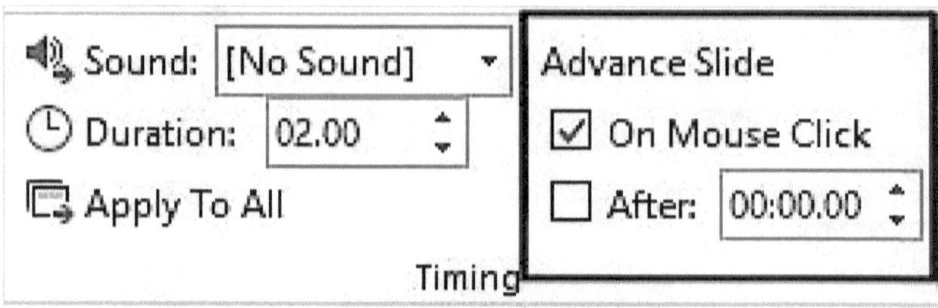

- Deselect the checkbox for "On Mouse Click" because we want the photo album to progress through each picture automatically without needing our input.

- Check the box for "After" and modify the value using the up and down arrows to 6 seconds. You can choose any length of time you desire, input a value, and test it before settling on a final duration.

- To apply this setting to all slides in the photo album, click the "Apply To All" button.

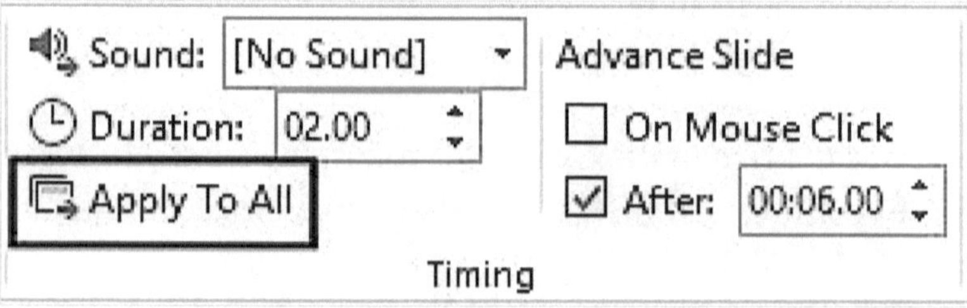

- To initiate the slideshow, press the F5 key on your keyboard and avoid clicking the mouse or pressing any key to see if the slides transition automatically based on the settings.

- As a final step, we want the presentation to loop back to the beginning after displaying the last slide. To do this, navigate to the Slide Show tab on the Ribbon and select Set Up Slide Show. In the Show options section, mark the box for Loop continuously until 'Esc' and click OK.

- If you are satisfied with the timing of the slideshow, save the file to your preferred location with an appropriate filename by pressing Ctrl + S on your keyboard. Your photo album is now complete and ready to be used at your next event. You can showcase the presentation using a data projector or by connecting your computer to your TV and playing the slideshow. Refer to your TV's manual for instructions.

I hope you found this tutorial helpful in creating a photo album using PowerPoint.

17

Create a "Your own adventure" storybook in PowerPoint

The PowerPoint Edge - Mastering the Art of Storytelling

Throughout my experience in providing professional development for educators, I have had the chance to showcase the various ways in which PowerPoint can be utilized to engage students. One exciting exercise is creating an interactive story that allows users to guide the story and achieve a different ending each time. As a child, I loved the "choose your own adventure" book series, and this concept can be replicated in PowerPoint.

To create this type of interactive storybook, it is crucial to map out your story options. By the end of development, you could have anywhere from a dozen to a hundred slides, each with different parts of your story. You want to make sure that you don't confuse yourself and that your story progresses coherently for readers.

Steps to get started:

- Open Microsoft PowerPoint.

- Create a new blank presentation.

- Click on the placeholder to add a title for your story and include your author details in the subtitle area.

The PowerPoint Edge - Mastering the Art of Storytelling

- It's worth noting that the PowerPoint Design Ideas feature can suggest design ideas for your opening slide. Feel free to apply them whenever you wish.

- Next, we should insert a new slide to commence our story.

- Either click on the "New Slide" button located on the "Home" tab or press "Ctrl + M" on your keyboard.

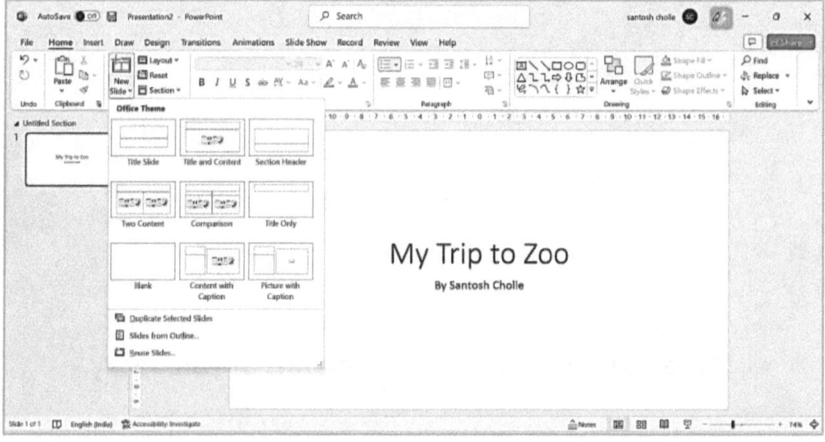

- Select the slide layout with a Title and Content section, which will enable us to create a chapter title and write the initial paragraphs of our story.

- To create a chapter title, click on the text box that reads "Click to add title."

- Enter your chapter title.

- Next, click on the main text box where you will see the message "Click to add text."

- Since I don't want to use bullet points in my story, I will turn off this feature by clicking on the Bullets button once on the Home tab of the Ribbon.

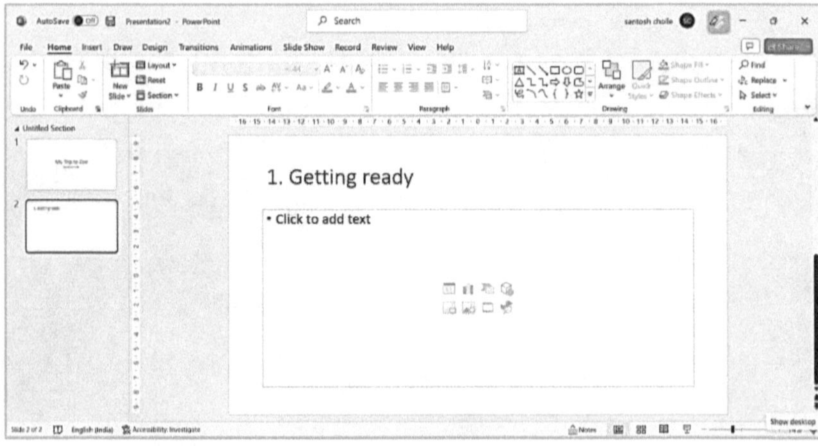

- Type the first couple of paragraphs of your story.

- End the first part of your story at the point where the reader will need to make their first decision.

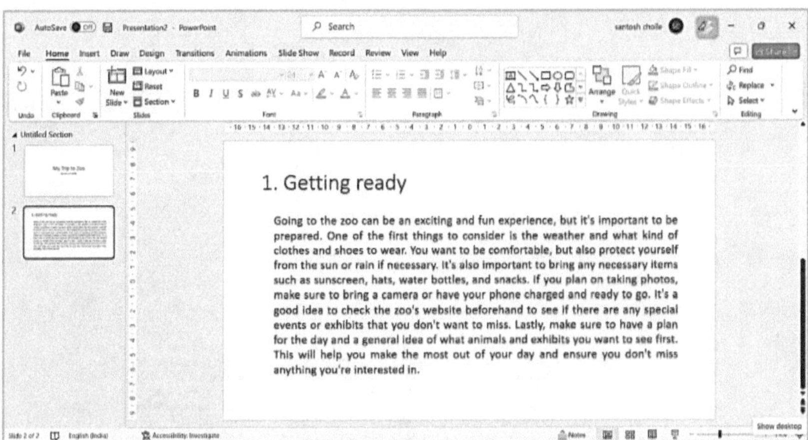

Create the first story choice

- To create the first story choice, start by clicking on the "New Slide" button or using the keyboard shortcut "Ctrl + M."

- Then, add the chapter number and a title for this section of the story on the slide. This will help you keep track of the different parts of your story.

- Next, type in the next part of the story for choice 1.

- Repeat the previous steps to create the additional option for your story, which will show the result for choice 2.

- This will give you a total of four slides in your storybook, with readers choosing between two options on slide 2 that will take them to either slide 3 or slide 4.

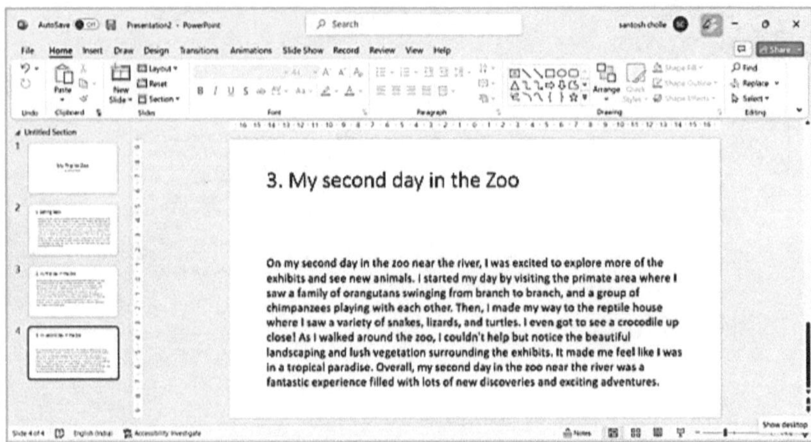

Create buttons to choose an option

To allow the reader to make a choice between options, we need to create buttons that will take them to a specific slide based on their selection.

- Start by selecting slide 2 where the reader needs to make a choice.

- Then, navigate to the Ribbon and click on the "Insert" tab.

- From here, select "Shapes" and scroll to the bottom of the gallery where you will find the "Action Buttons" section.

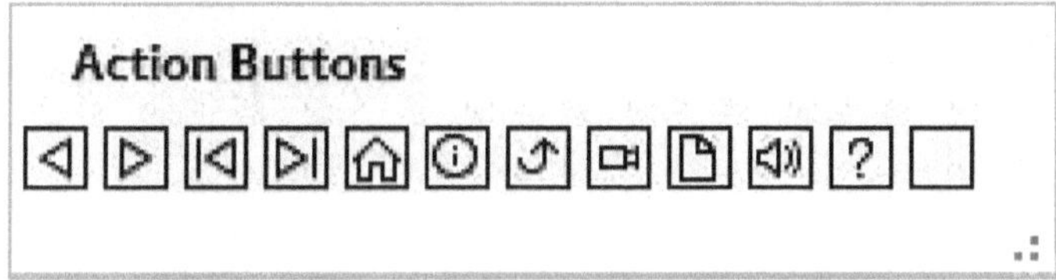

- Draw the blank Action Button onto the slide by selecting it from the Action Buttons section of the Shapes gallery.

- As soon as you have drawn the button onto the slide, the Action Settings dialog box will appear:

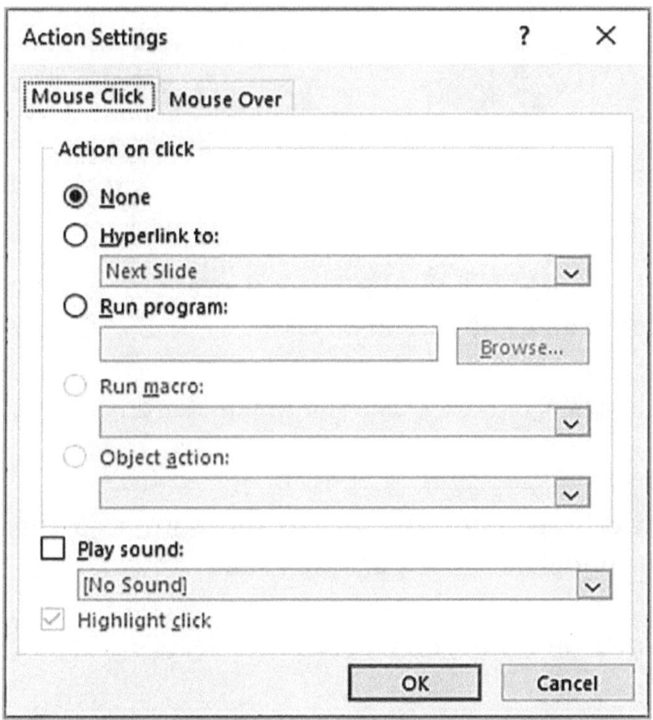

- Choose the option "Hyperlink to" from the given options.

- Select "Slide" from the drop-down menu.

- You will see a list of your slides, now choose the slide which contains the first-choice option for your story.

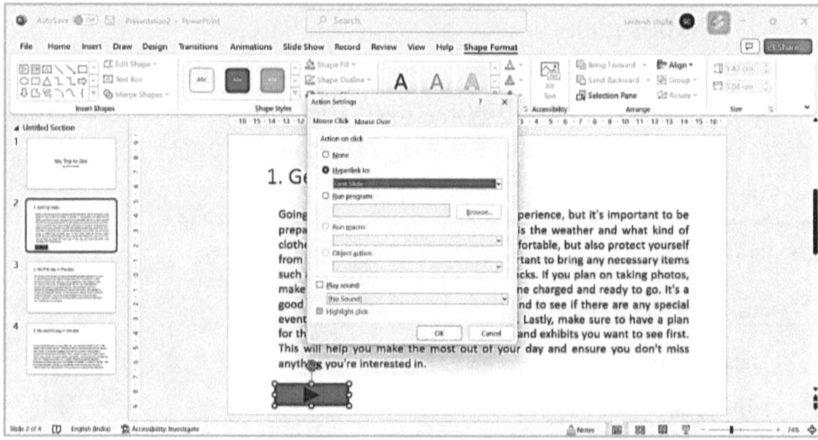

- For the purpose of this demonstration, I have selected slide 2 and clicked on OK.

- Click on OK again to close the Action Settings dialog box.

- The next step is to add text to the button so that readers understand the purpose of each option.

- Right-click on the action button and select Edit Text.

- Enter the title you gave for each story option to match up your slides and buttons.

- Repeat these steps to add the action button for the second story option.

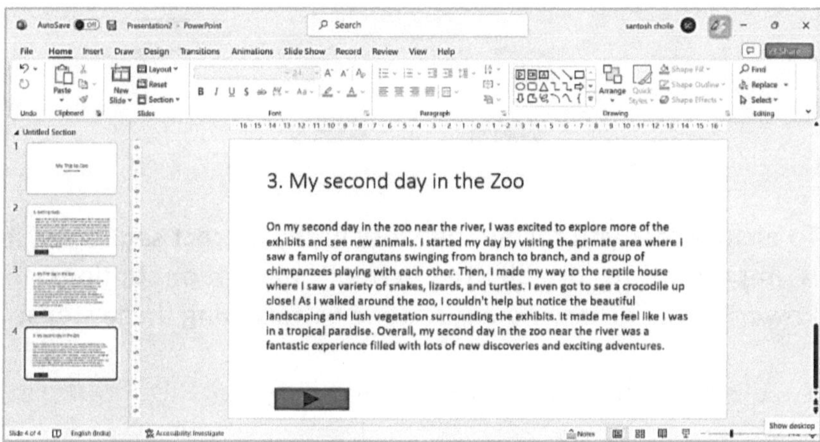

After completing the first part of the story and adding the first choice point, the next step is to repeat the process to add new storyline options to each slide. The level of complexity can be adjusted based on the desired number of options, and the use of action buttons allows for easy navigation through the story. By following this process, it's possible to create a storyline with as many choices as desired.

In this example, there are a total of 6 options available for readers to explore.

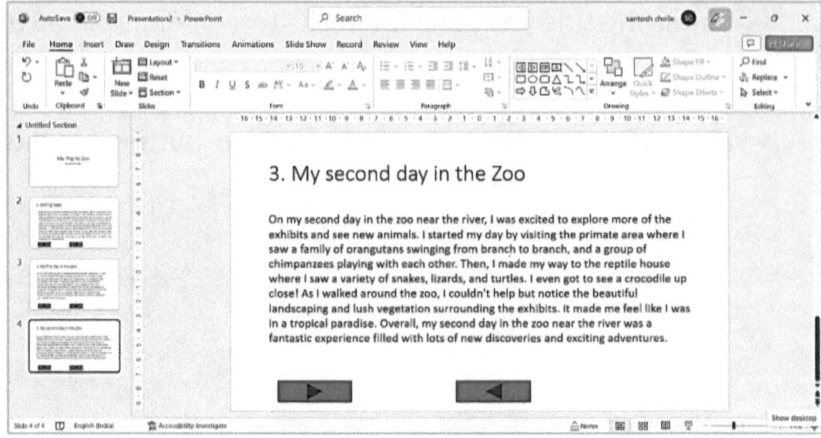

To ensure that you follow the story in the correct sequence, it is important to disable the default navigation options in PowerPoint. This can be easily done by following these steps:

- Go to the Transitions tab on the ribbon.

- Locate the Advance Slide section and uncheck the On Mouse Click option.

- This will prevent readers from moving through the presentation using the mouse, forcing them to use the action buttons to navigate through the story.

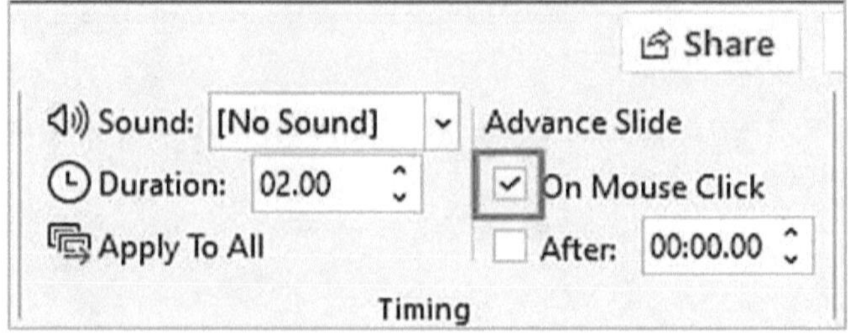

- To apply the kiosk setting to all slides, click the "Apply to All Slides" button.

By applying the kiosk setting, readers will not be able to use the keyboard to navigate through the presentation, which is important to ensure they experience the story in the intended order. Once the setting is applied, the presentation will automatically run in full-screen mode and readers will only be able to navigate through the story using the action buttons that have been set up. This helps to create an immersive and interactive experience for the reader, and ensures that they are fully engaged with the story.

- Go to the Slide Show tab on the ribbon

- Select Set Up Slide Show

- Under Show type, choose Browsed at a kiosk (full screen)

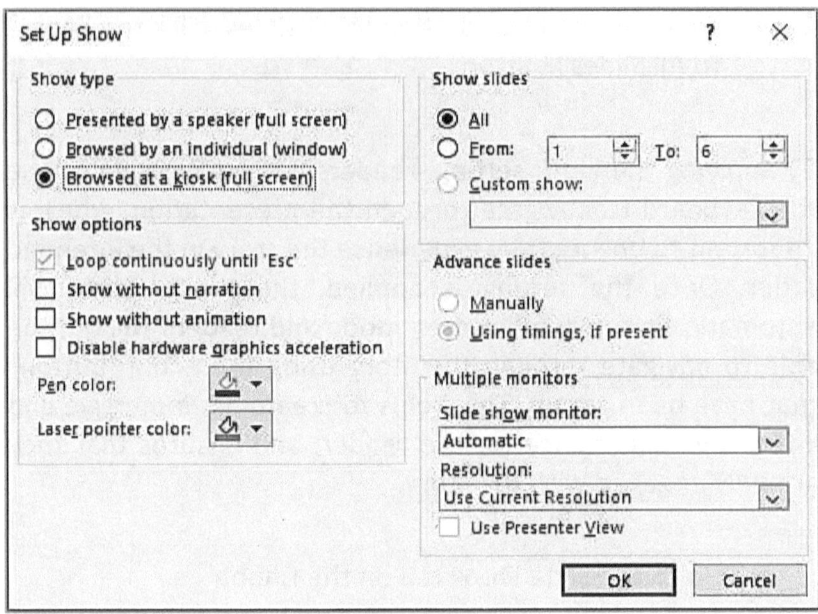

- Click OK. Since we have disabled the keyboard navigation, we need to add a button to the opening slide that readers can use to "start reading."

Follow the previous section's steps to create an action button on slide 1 that links to the first slide of your story.

Test Your Story

Now it's time to have some fun and test your story to ensure that it makes sense and flows correctly through the options.

- Press the F5 key on your keyboard to start the slide show.

- Use your action buttons to move through the story and ensure that they take you to the correct part of the story.

Make It Look Nice

My slides look boring, and you can quickly and easily add some colour using PowerPoint's built-in design themes.

- Click the Design tab on the ribbon.

- Hover your mouse over a design to see what your current slide will look like and explore the available design options.

- Simply click on the design to apply it.

- In my case, I downloaded a free PowerPoint template from SlidesCarnival.com and applied it by selecting the "Browse for Themes" option within the design gallery drop-down menu.

To ensure you don't lose any progress, it's important to save your storybook as a PowerPoint file (.pptx) as you work on it. This will allow you to make changes and edits in the future if necessary.

However, if you want to distribute your storybook to readers while preventing them from editing the content or action buttons, it's best to save it as a slide show file. Here's how:

- Press the F12 key on your keyboard to perform the Save As function.

- The Save As window will appear.

- Choose the location where you want to save the file.

- If necessary, change the file name.

- Select the Save as type drop-down menu and choose PowerPoint Show (.ppsx) from the options.

- Click Save. Your file storybook is now complete, and you can distribute it to your students.

- However, the PPSX file we created may not work correctly in Microsoft Teams as students may be able to navigate through the story using the mouse, rendering the story incomprehensible.

- This issue was discovered during the writing of this segment, and after contacting Microsoft Support, it was revealed to be a "by design" feature. To address this problem, it is recommended that you add this issue to the Teams UserVoice website and vote for it to be fixed so that a PPSX file cannot be browsed using the mouse in Teams.

18

3D Model Animations in PowerPoint 365

One of my sessions, named "3D Model Animations in PowerPoint 365," has been a challenging task for me to fit in the given 30-minute time slot in the Office365 Training Lab. Although there are various exciting features that can be explored with 3D models in PowerPoint, I have limited it to some crucial aspects.

Where to find 3D models

For those of us who lack artistic skills, finding pre-made 3D models can be a daunting task. Luckily, there are several websites where artists can upload their 3D models for others to download and use.

One such website was Remix 3D, which was previously offered by Microsoft. However, it was discontinued in January 2020. But don't worry, you can still insert 3D models directly into PowerPoint.

Another website option is Google Poly, which allows users to download 3D models to their local computers for use in PowerPoint slides. There are also many other websites available if you perform a quick search. Alternatively, you can use the Paint 3D app, which comes as part of Windows 10, to create your own 3D models.

If you want to insert a 3D model from a stock library, the old Remix 3D website has been replaced by a stock 3D model library. Here's how to do it:

- Open Microsoft PowerPoint 365 and create a new blank presentation.

The PowerPoint Edge - Mastering the Art of Storytelling

- Insert a new blank slide (Ctrl + M) or change the first slide to the Blank slide layout.

- Click the Insert tab and select 3D Models.

- From the drop-down menu, choose Stock 3D Models.

- The Online 3D Models window will appear.

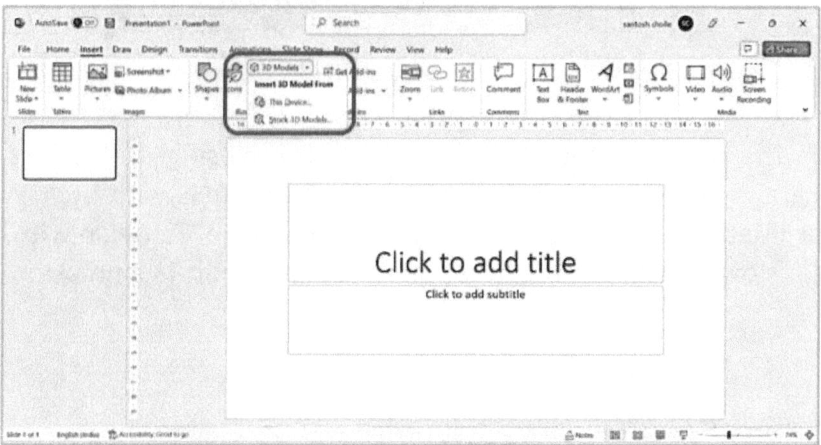

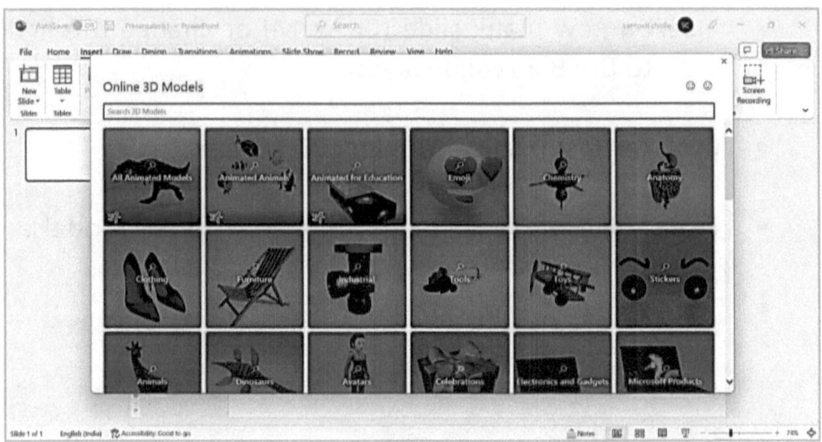

In the provided search box or through browsing the various categories, you can look for 3D models. Models with built-in animation are marked with a running man icon. To begin with, let's explore a 3D model that does not have built-in animation.

Non-Animated

Animated

- To insert a 3D model, select the desired model and click on the "Insert" button.

- Allow it a few moments to download.

- The 3D model will appear on the slide.

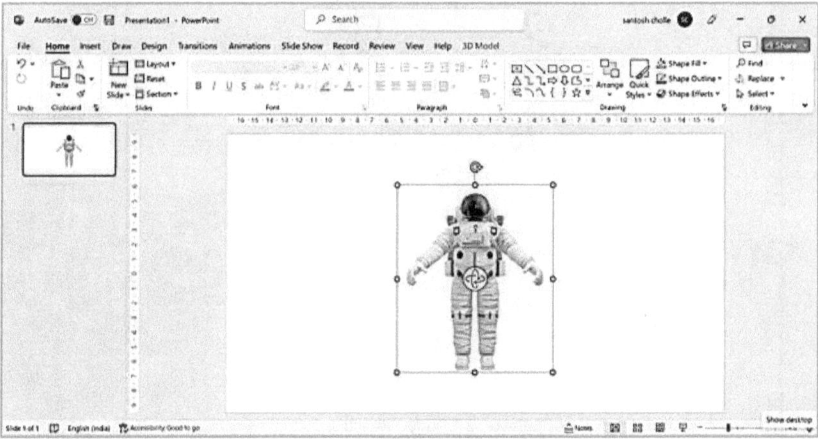

Resize a 3D Model

To resize the model to suit your slide, use the corner resize handles displayed around the 3D Model.

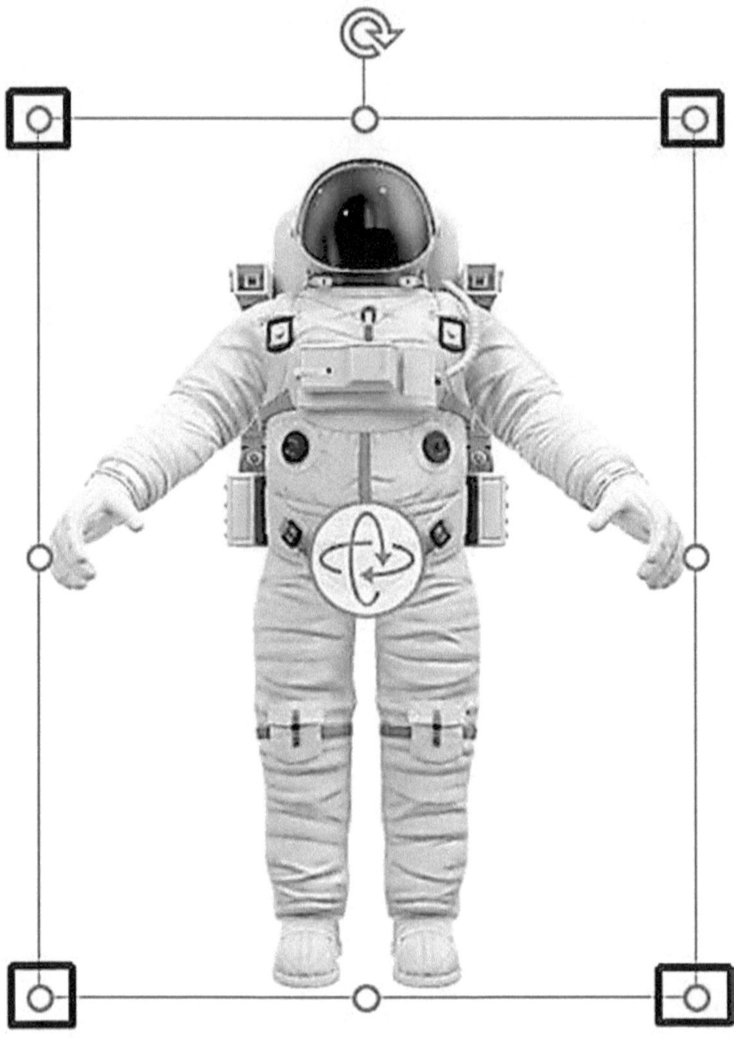

You also have the option of utilizing the "Size" category found in the 3D Model contextual tab.

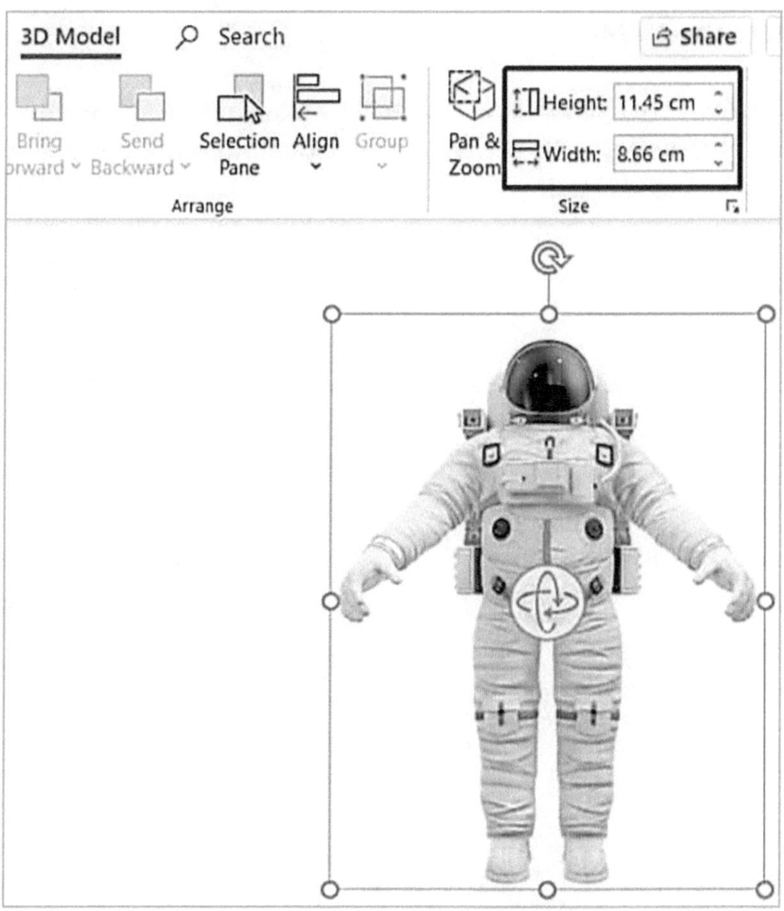
3D Model
Search
Share
Bring
Forward
Send
Backward
Selection
Pane
Align
Group
Pan &
Zoom
Height: 11.45 cm
Width: 8.66 cm
Arrange
Size

Rotate the 3D Model

If you want to showcase a specific angle of the 3D model, simply employ the 3D control button located in the middle of the model to rotate it.

Animate a 3D Model

In PowerPoint, it's possible to add animation effects to your 3D models. In addition to the pre-installed effects, you will find a selection of new 3D animation effects that are specifically designed for 3D models. These effects include "arrive," "turntable," "swing," "jump & turn," and "leave."

To apply one of these animation effects, follow these steps:

- Ensure that the 3D model is selected.

- Navigate to the "Animations" tab on the Ribbon.

- Click on the "More" button in the Animation gallery to access all available animation effects.

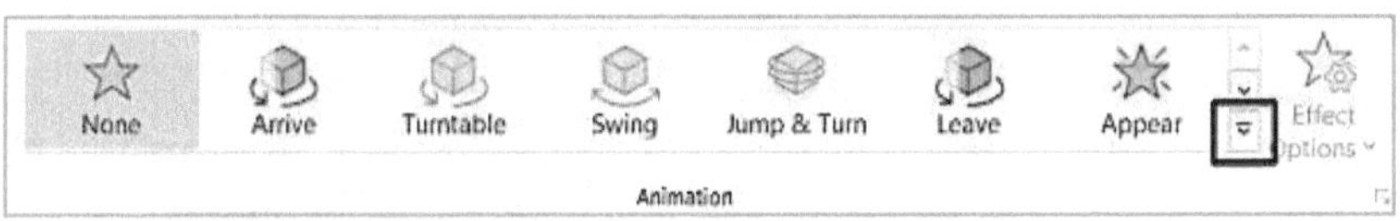

- Locate the "3D" group of effects.

- Choose an effect from the available options; for example, I'll select the "Turntable" effect.

- The animation preview should begin.

- Access the "Timing" group on the Ribbon to view the "Duration" setting, which is currently set to 20 seconds.

- The current duration is too long for the astronaut to turn around, so I want to make it faster.

- Adjust the "Duration" setting to 8 seconds.

- Click on the "Preview" button on the left side of the Animations tab to preview the changes.

- This speed is more suitable, but feel free to continue adjusting until you achieve your desired result.

Let's now add another animation that involves the astronaut jumping and spinning. To make the process more manageable, let's display the Animation Pane.

- Click on the "Animation Pane" button found in the Animations tab.

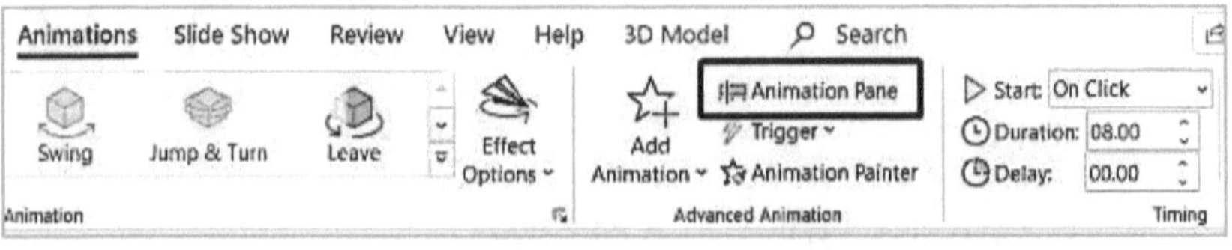

- With the Animation Pane now visible on the right side of the screen, we can proceed to add a second animation to the astronaut.

- Select the 3D model and click on the "Add Animation" button located to the left of the Animation Pane button.

- From the list of available animations, choose the "3D > Jump and Turn" effect.

- The astronaut now has a second animation, which is listed in the Animation Pane.

- As before, adjust the "Duration" setting to slow down or speed up the "jump and turn" animation.

Set the Animation to automatically start

If you preview these animation effects in Slide Show mode by pressing F5 on the keyboard, nothing will happen until you click the mouse or press a key. Ideally, the animations should occur automatically without prompting.

To make our animations play automatically one after the other, we need to change the "Start" setting in the "Timing" group. By default, the Start settings are set to "On Click," which requires a mouse click or key press to activate the animation. We want both animations to occur automatically.

- Select the first animation in the Animation Pane.

- From the Animations tab, change the "Start" setting to "After Previous."

- Repeat step 2 for the second animation.

Even though nothing is happening before the first animation, PowerPoint considers the slide being displayed on the screen as an "action," triggering the first animation to start.

Press F5 again to preview the animations in Slide Show mode, and ensure that they play automatically without intervention.

Insert an Animated 3D Model

The Remix 3D gallery provides some pre-animated 3D models that feature impressive levels of detail. These are always fun to work with. For free stock images, you can check out Pexels.com.

- Insert a new blank slide by pressing Ctrl + M on the keyboard.

- Firstly, add the desired background image by clicking on "Design" and then "Format Background."

- The Format Background pane will appear.

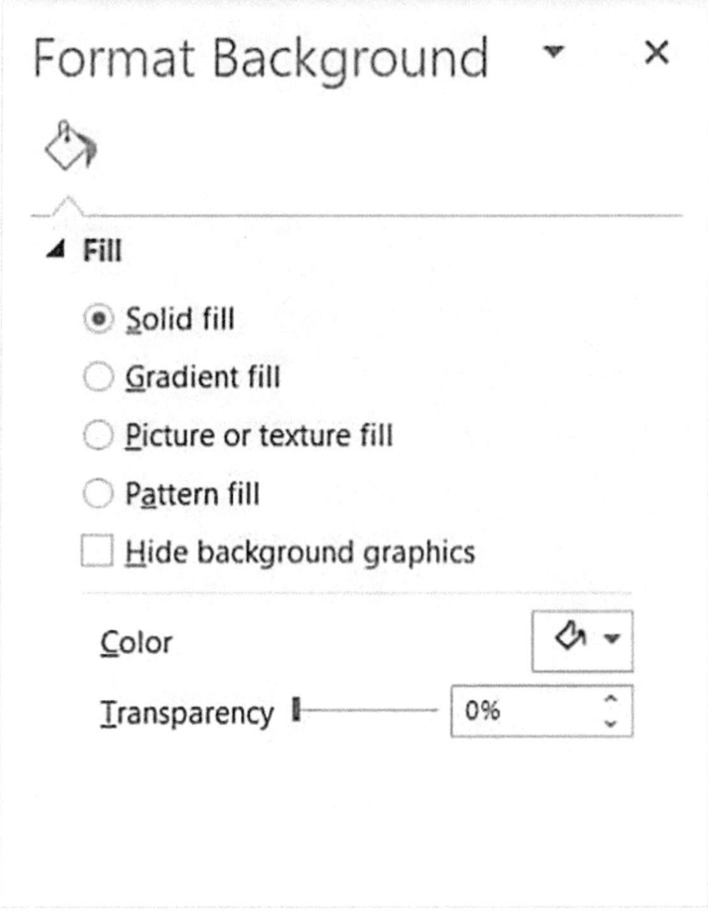

- Choose the "Picture or texture fill" option from the "Fill" menu.

- Use the "File" button to add your desired picture from your computer.

- Pick the image you want to use as the background and click "Open."

- The selected image will now appear as the background on your slide.

- To insert our animated 3D model, navigate to the "Insert" tab and select "3D Models."

- From the dropdown menu, choose "From Online Sources."

- This will bring up the "Online 3D Models" window.

- From the available categories, select "All Animated Models."

- Take a look at the animated model options to see what's available. For this example, we'll use the Dog.

- Click on the Dog model, then click the "Insert" button located in the bottom right corner.

- The 3D model will now be added to your slide.

- You can adjust the size and rotation of the model just as you would with a static 3D model.

- If you select the model, the animation will start automatically. A "Play/Pause" button will appear on the 3D model, which allows you to control the animation's activity.

Next, we'll add some extra animation effects to create the illusion that the Dogis charging toward us.

3D Model Scenes

In addition to their animations, 3D models often come with built-in scenes that offer different movement options. For instance, the Dog model offers five different scenes to choose from, including running (scene 1), crouching and looking around (scene 2), stopping and roaring (scene 3), flipping its tail and roaring (scene 4), or standing and looking around (scene 5).

To switch between scenes:

- Select the animated 3D model on your slide.

- Go to the "3D Model" tab in the ribbon.

- Click the "Scenes" button (second from the left) and pick a different scene option.

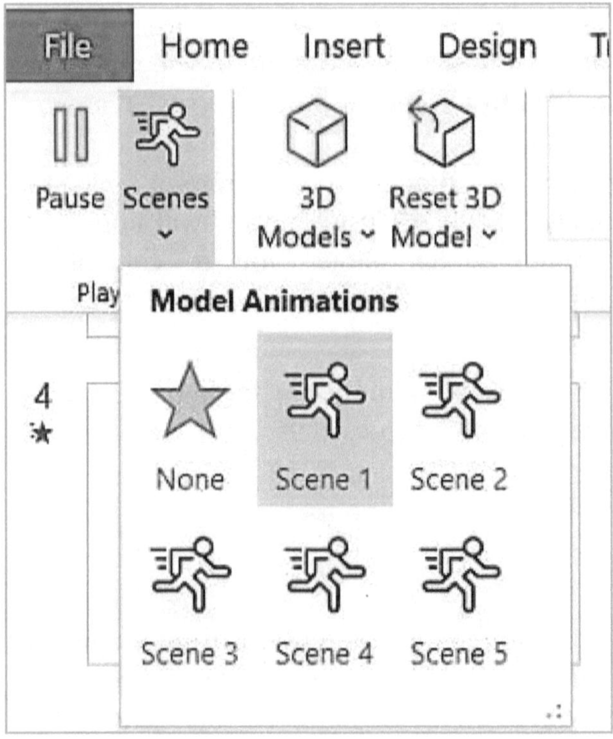

Let's return to the "Scenes" button and explore the other scene options.

Animating your 3D model:

Now we'll add some animations to our already-animated 3D model to create the illusion that it's running toward us.

- I'll position the Dog at the far end of the dirt road and resize it to fit. As it runs toward us, we want it to increase in size.

- Keep the "Animation Pane" visible for ease of use during this process.

- You should see that the 3D model already has an animation for the scene, which needs to be there for the running animation to be included in the sequence. If you accidentally delete it, select the model, click the "3D Models" tab, then click "Scenes" and choose "Scene 1" again to add it back into the Animation Pane sequence.

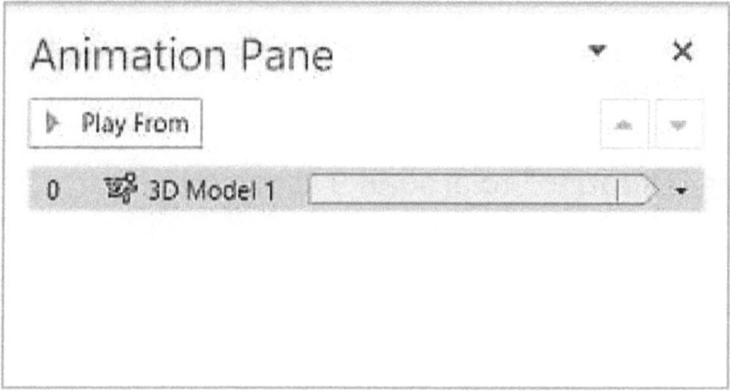

- Access the "Animations" tab on the Ribbon.

- Click the "Add Animation" button.

- Scroll through the options and find "Motion Paths." I'll be using the "Custom Path" option to guide my Dog through the slight bend in the road. This may require some practice. Alternatively, you can use the "Line" motion path to make the Dog run in a straight line.

- Once you've selected the "Motion Path," use your mouse to draw a path from the Dog to the road closest to the front. To complete the "Custom Path," double-click your mouse.

- You'll now see a preview of your custom path. Don't worry about the speed yet.

- Change the "Start" setting for the animation to "With Previous."

- Slow down the "Motion Path" animation so that the Dog moves at a slower pace.

- Select the "Custom Path" animation from the Animation Pane.

- Adjust the "Duration" to around 9 seconds.

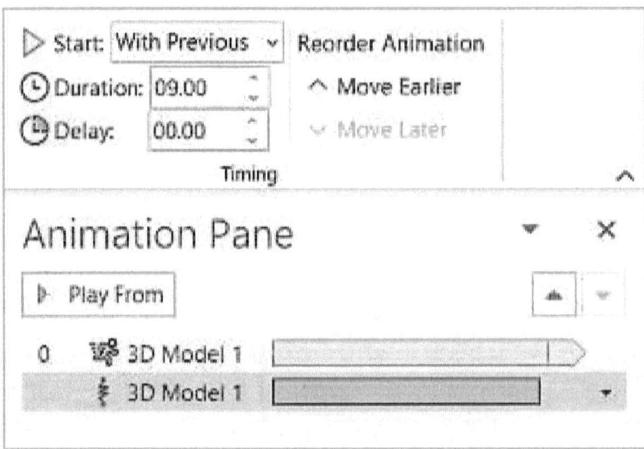

Previewing the animation using Alt + F5.

To create the illusion that the Dog is growing in size as it runs towards us, we will use the Grow/Shrink animation effect.

- Click on the 3D Model and go to the Animations tab. Click on the Add Animation button.

- Choose the Grow/Shrink effect.

- The Animation Pane will display three animations.

- Set the Start setting to With Previous to synchronize all animations.

- Set the duration to the same 09.00 seconds as the previous animation.

- Preview the animation by pressing Alt + F5.

- If the Dog doesn't appear to have grown enough, click on the drop-down arrow located on the right of the Grow/Shrink effect and select Effect Options.

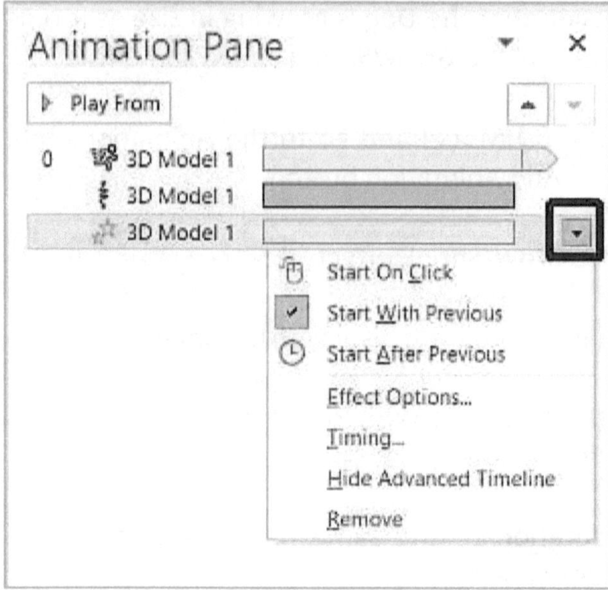

- My next step is to modify the Size parameter of the Grow/Shrink effect to make the Dog appear larger. I will increase it to 250% and press the Enter key, then click OK to apply the changes.

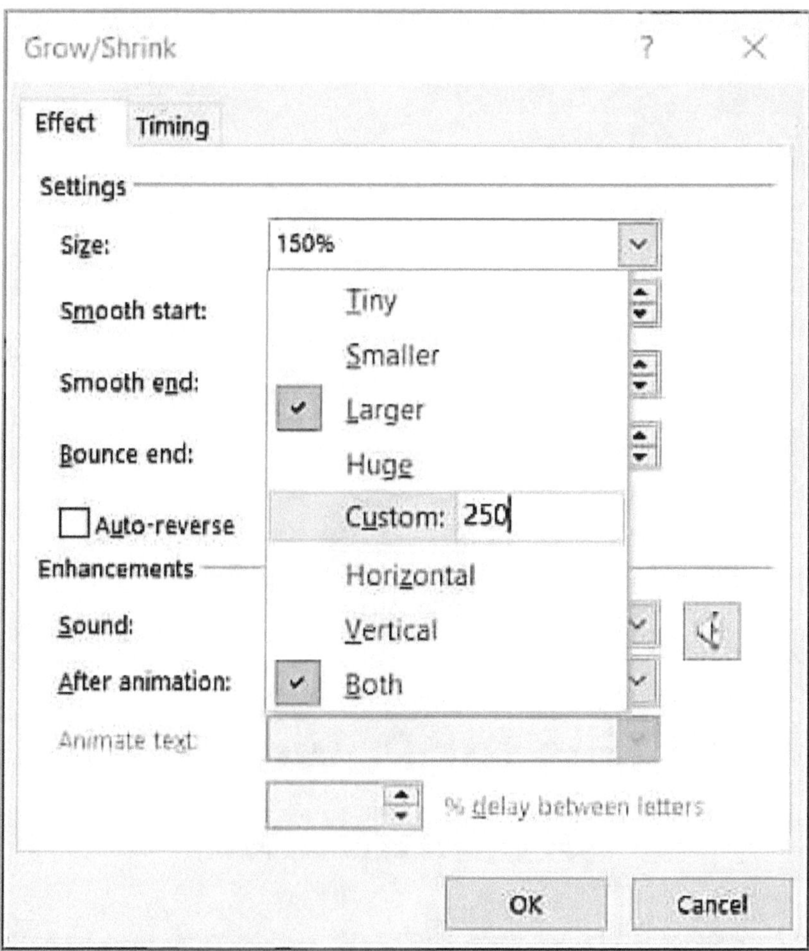

- Preview the animation once more by pressing Alt + F5.
- Congratulations, your 3D Model animation is now finished.

Feel free to experiment with other animation effects to see what you can create.

19

10 Tips for PowerPoint presentation

Microsoft PowerPoint is a feature-rich program that can be used to create engaging presentations. However, just like many people, you may have experienced a dull and tedious presentation that made you want to fall asleep. In this segment, I will share my top 10 tips for creating a captivating PowerPoint presentation that will keep your audience engaged.

✓ Tip 1: Keep it simple

This is a fundamental tip that you will often come across when searching for presentation ideas online. While PowerPoint offers many fun and exciting tools, it's crucial to keep things simple. Avoid using too many animations, flashy font colours, or in-depth bullet points that can distract your audience. Remember, the primary purpose of a PowerPoint presentation is to complement the information you're delivering verbally.

✓ Tip 2: Avoid distracting background images

While background images can add visual interest to your slides, it's essential to choose images that do not interfere with the readability of your content. If you decide to use a background image, make sure it has a washed-out or transparent effect to make your slide content easy to read.

Avoid using frivolous or distracting background images that could hinder the readability of the information presented on your slide.

✓ Tip 3: Embrace white space

Some PowerPoint users think that they need to fill every inch of a slide to make it appear balanced or to avoid it looking empty. However, this is not true. The principle of "less is more" applies to PowerPoint presentations as well, so keep the content on each slide to a minimum. Your presentation should not be a word-for-word transcript of what you're going to say. Instead, include only the essential facts or aspects that you want to highlight during each slide. Embracing white space can make your presentation easier to read and more visually appealing.

✓ Tip 4: Use animations and slide transitions sparingly

Although animations and slide transitions can add value to many PowerPoint presentations and are certainly entertaining to create, it's important to avoid the temptation of animating every object, heading, or bullet point on every slide. Use these features judiciously and only when they serve to enhance or clarify your content, rather than just showing off your proficiency with PowerPoint.

✓ Tip 5: Choose high-quality images

Images can greatly enhance the topic of discussion on a slide and speak volumes, but it's essential to use high-quality images that improve rather than detract from your content. While it's easy to conduct a quick Google image search and grab whatever you need, it's important to respect the copyright of these images. Instead, use professional images or "stock images" that will provide a more professional and effective image to any slide.

You can source images from internal company sources such as your marketing department or online sources, including stock image websites. Better yet, if possible, use your own digital camera to experiment with creating the exact image you want to use. An original image is much better than a random image from the Internet.

✓ Tip 6: Opt for the Right Colour Scheme

Selecting an appropriate colour scheme is a crucial aspect of designing any presentation. Sometimes, corporate entities will dictate a set of colours through style guides, thus removing this decision from the design process. However, if you are not restricted by corporate colours, you should decide on a colour scheme at the start of the design process.

Would you opt for a dark background with light text or a light background with dark text? Whichever option you choose, it is essential to ensure that the background colour and colours used for text and objects contrast with each other.

A useful guide that can help with colour selection is the "Psychological Properties of Colours" guide by Colour Effects.co.uk. This guide outlines popular colours and the psychological effects they can have on people.

✓ Tip 7: Pick the Right Font

Choosing a font for your presentation may come down to personal preference, but you should consider your audience's perspective while designing your presentation. Will the font style be easy to read on the screen?

Using a Sans Serif font style is often more legible on a screen than a traditional Serif font style. Here are examples of both font types:

Serif fonts	Sans Serif fonts
Cambria, Garamond, Georgia, and Times New Roman	Arial Calibri Tahoma Trebuchet MS

Similar to how font colours have a psychological effect, the type of font you choose can also evoke different responses.

✓ **Tip 8: Keep the number of slides in check**

When designing your presentation, it's crucial to limit the number of slides to ensure you have enough time to cover all the content effectively. The number of slides you create should be proportional to the time you have, with 1-2 minutes per slide being a good rule of thumb. Including too many slides will result in a rushed presentation, while having too few may leave you with extra time and nothing to discuss. To determine the ideal number of slides, it's advisable to use the Rehearse Timings feature of PowerPoint, which allows you to test out the timing of your slides and the content you plan to discuss.

✓ **Tip 9: Create your own design template**

Although PowerPoint offers several built-in design templates, using them can make your presentation appear unprofessional and overused. To create a more effective message, it's best to develop your own design template using PowerPoint. It's easy to do, and there are numerous websites where you can download both free and paid templates if you don't feel confident creating your own.

✓ **Tip 10: Check your spelling and grammar**

Nothing can detract from your message more than a spelling or grammar error in your presentation. Even if you catch the mistake, you can be certain that your audience has noticed it as well. To avoid such errors, run multiple spell checks on your slides and have a colleague or friend proofread them as well. Additionally, look for errors that PowerPoint may not catch, such as incorrect word usage or context.

I trust that these tips provide a solid foundation for starting your presentation design process. If you're looking for further guidance on utilizing PowerPoint effectively.

20

Bonus Tip - Microsoft Sway

How to create a digital presentation using Microsoft Sway

During one of my sessions, I had the pleasure of presenting and demonstrated how to use Microsoft Sway. To provide attendees with additional resources, I will be narrating a series of segments containing information from my sessions, as well as some tips and tricks.

This particular segment will focus on Microsoft Sway, which is a fun program to work with. Let's get started by discussing what Sway is all about.

What is Microsoft Sway?

Microsoft Sway is an application that was launched in 2015 to help users create and share presentations, newsletters, stories, and more. Sway is content-centered, which means you can focus solely on the content and story you are telling, without the need for all the bells and whistles that you get from other programs like PowerPoint. Sway includes a built-in design feature that lets you quickly style your presentation without spending hours trying to make it look polished.

Microsoft Sway is suitable for both classroom and business settings, and its applications and uses are limitless.

How to Launch Microsoft Sway

There are two ways to use Microsoft Sway. Firstly, you can install and use the desktop app, or you can log in to the online portal and work via your web browser.

Installing the Sway App

The Sway app is available through the Microsoft Store. However, if you are using an Apple or Android device, there is no compatible app available, so you will need to access Sway through your web browser. Here are the steps to install the Sway desktop app:

- Click the Start button on your computer and locate the Microsoft Store.

- Once the Microsoft Store is displayed, click the Search button in the top right corner and type "Sway".

- From the results, locate the Apps section, and Sway will likely be the first app listed.

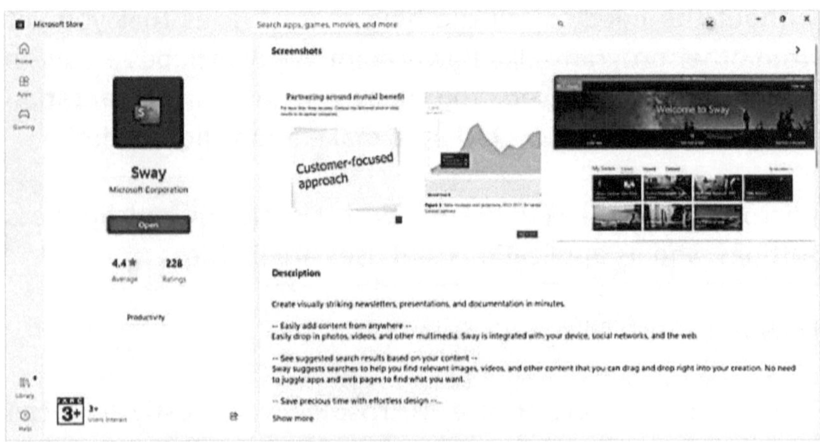

Installing Sway App:

- Click on the app to view more details, and then click the "Get" button.

- The Sway app will be installed on your computer.

- After the installation is complete, click the "Launch" button or locate the app in your Start menu.

- The Sway start screen will be displayed.

Using Sway via Web Browser:

If you prefer to use Sway through your web browser, follow these steps:

- Open your preferred web browser.

- Enter the address https://sway.office.com/ and hit enter.

- Click the link to log in using your Microsoft account.

- The Sway start screen will be displayed.

Although I prefer using the Sway app, having access to the online version is great when I'm away from my computer.

Creating Your First Sway:

Microsoft Sway is based on two main elements: the Storyline and Cards. The Storyline represents the sequencing of your information, while cards are the different types of elements you can include.

Let's create a Sway from scratch:

- Click "Create New" from the Sway screen.

- A new Sway will be displayed, with a Heading card already added.

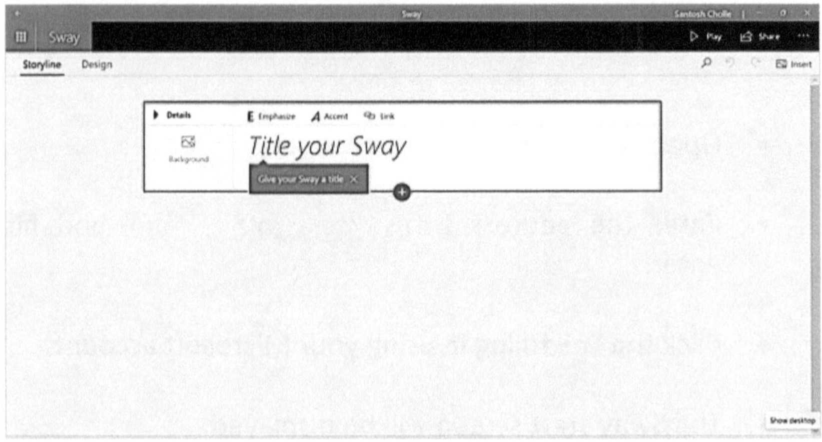

- Type in a Title for your Sway.

- If you want to add an image as the background behind your title, you can include a Background in the Heading card.

- Click the Background image button located within the Heading card.

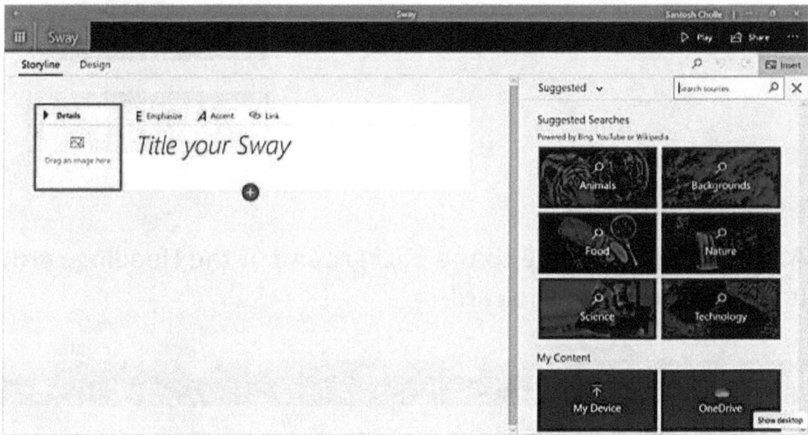

You will now see various options to add images. You can either use the "Suggested" drop-down menu to search specific sources, or select the "My Device" option at the bottom to upload content from your own computer.

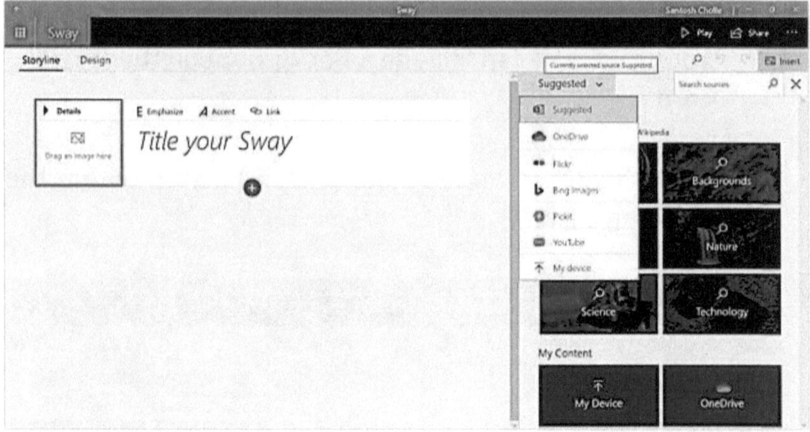

After adding an image to the background of the Heading card, it will be shown on the card.

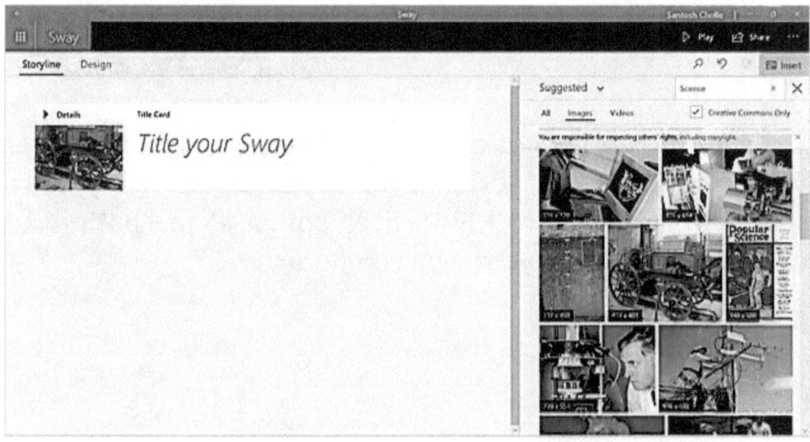

Creating a Text Card

Now that you have set up your Heading Card, let's add some content into your Sway by creating a Text Card.

- Click on the "Insert Content" button located at the bottom of the first Heading Card.

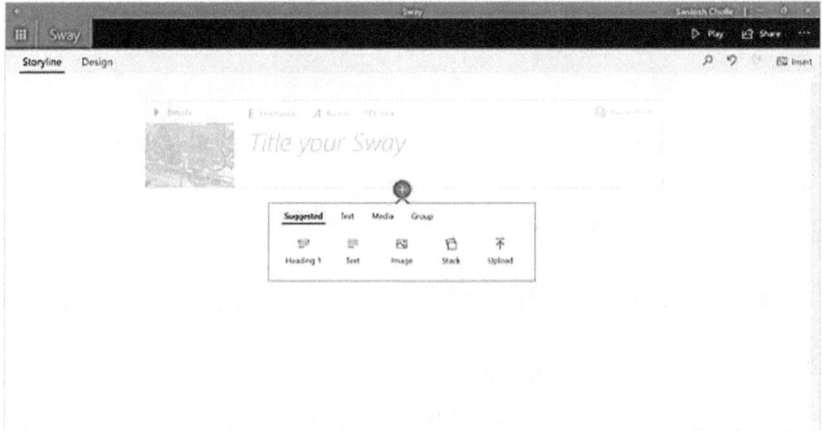

- Choose the option "Text" from the available card options.

- This will result in a new card being displayed for adding text content.

- Type in the content you want to display in the presentation inside the **Text** card by placing the cursor within the card.

- The toolbar within the Text card allows you to switch to a **Heading** card by clicking the **Heading** button, and apply formatting styles such as **Emphasiz**e and **Accent**. You can also use **Bullets** and **Numbers** to display lists or instructions, and the **Link** button to add a hyperlink with a text placeholder.

- On the right side of the **Text** card toolbar, you can find three buttons: **Subtle, Moderate, and Delete**.

- The **Subtle** and **Moderate** buttons enable you to change the size of the card within the presentation, while the **Delete** button allows you to remove the card. Preview your Sway

Preview your Sway

To preview your Sway presentation after making changes, click the Play button located on the top menu bar.

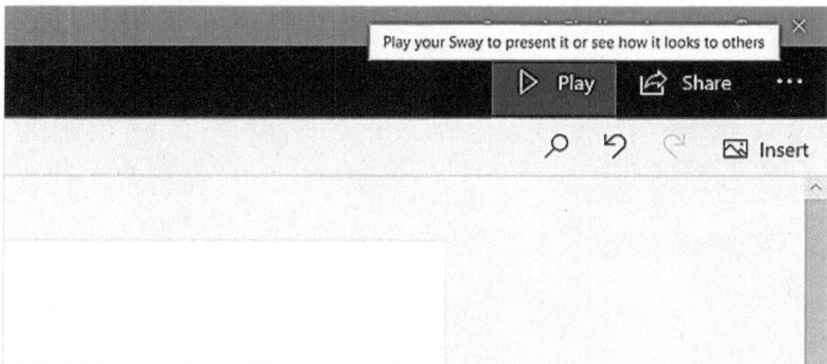

Add an Image card

To enhance the visual appeal of your presentation, you can add images to your Text card. For instance, if your content is about learning the alphabet, and you have a Text card for the letter "A," you can add images of objects that start with that letter.

Here's how to do it:

- Hover your cursor over the Text card, and click the **Insert Content** button (+).

- Choose **Image** from the available options.

- The Image card will appear, ready for you to add an image.

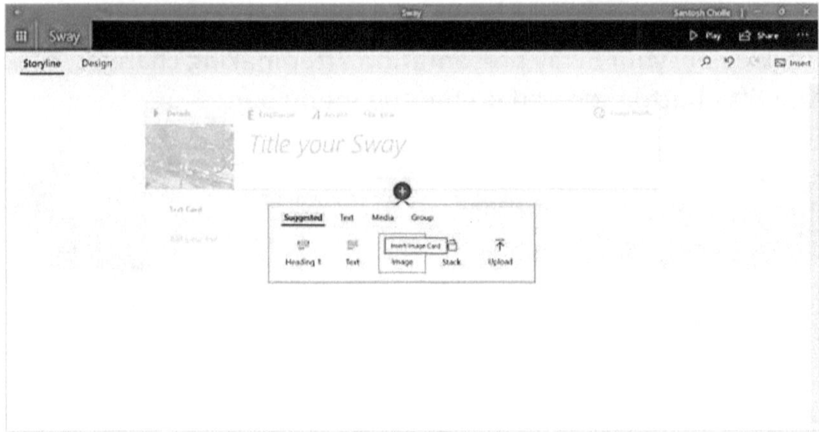

- As before, the side panel will appear and provide you with the option to search for images using the suggested sources or from your own device, just as when we added the background to the Heading card.

- Since I have saved images on my computer, I will choose the "My Device" option.

- Find and select the image you want to upload.

- Repeat the process to add two more images to complement your first text card.

- You should now have one text card and three image cards.

Style your Sway

To style your Sway presentation, you can make use of the built-in style gallery, which allows you to easily switch between different styles until you find the one that suits your preferences.

Here's how to do it:

- Go to the "**Design**" tab in the "**Storyline**" view.

- At this point, you can choose how you want your Sway to be displayed - whether it should scroll vertically, horizontally or as slides.

- The available style options can also be seen from this view.

- Each row in the style gallery represents a core style set with variations in fonts and colours.

- If you're feeling adventurous, you can click the "**Remix**" button, and Sway will randomly pick a style combination for you and display your Sway using that styling.

- Keep clicking the "**Remix**" button until you find a style that you like.

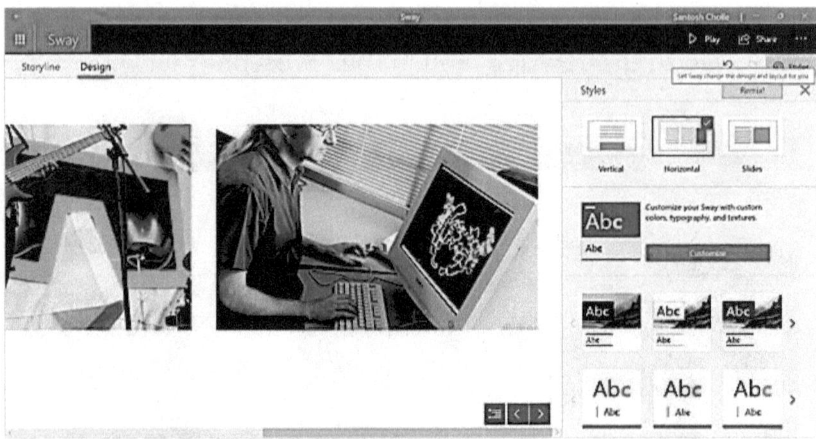

Share your Sway

Once you are happy with your Sway you are ready to share it with others. You have the option of sharing only within your organisation or school, specific people or groups or open it up for anyone to access your Sway.

To share your Sway with others, you can follow these steps:

- Open your Sway and locate the "Share" button on the main toolbar.

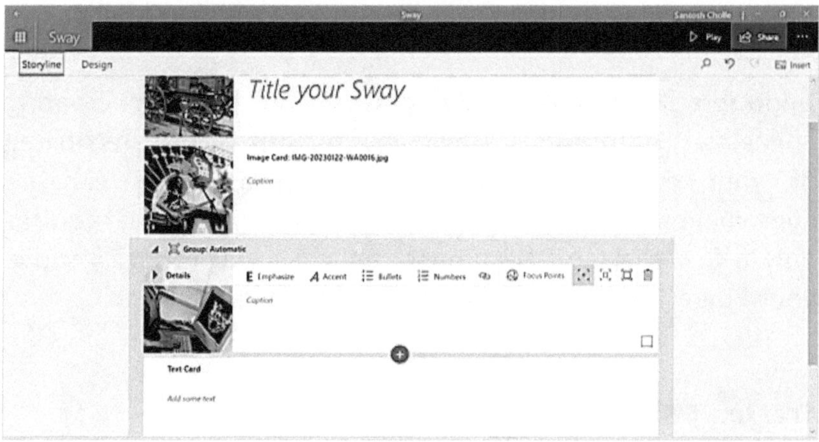

Congratulations on successfully creating your first Sway presentation. Now it's time to share it with others. You have the option to share your Sway within your organization or school, with specific individuals or groups, or make it accessible to anyone.

To share your Sway, click on the "Share" button located on the main toolbar. From the options provided, select who you want to share your Sway with. You can also choose if you want people to view or edit your Sway. Afterward, copy the link provided and share it via email or your preferred method.

Great job on getting started with Sway. Keep an eye out for more posts on using Sway, and click on the link provided to view more presentations from the Leading a Digital School Conference.

How to convert PowerPoint to Microsoft Sway

Undoubtedly, Microsoft Sway is a fun tool for creating engaging presentations. However, the idea of transferring all of your current content into Microsoft Sway can be overwhelming. Fortunately, this process is simple and requires only a few clicks of the mouse, allowing you to easily move your PowerPoint presentations into Microsoft Sway.

Create a Sway from PowerPoint

- To create a new Sway from an existing PowerPoint presentation, first open Microsoft Sway online at sway.office.com or launch the desktop app from the Start menu (I will be using the desktop app).

- If prompted, log in using your username and password.

- Once you're logged in, the main window of Microsoft Sway will appear.

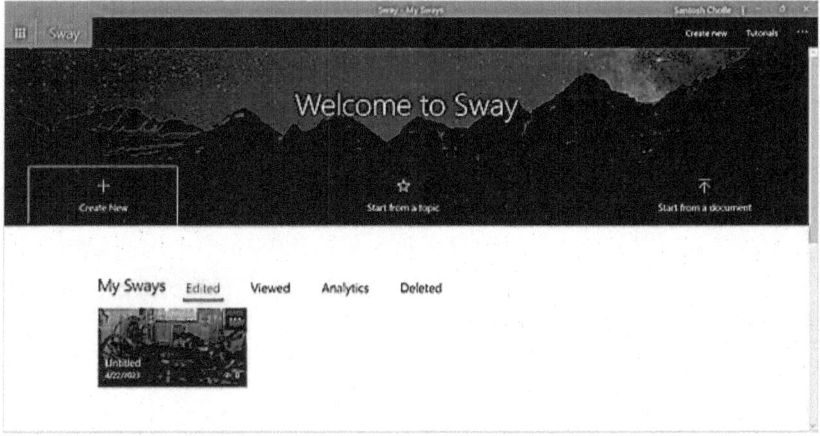

- Select "Start from a document" from the menu bar.

- Click on "Start from a document" from the menu bar to open the "Open" dialog box.

The PowerPoint Edge - Mastering the Art of Storytelling

- Navigate your local computer to select the PowerPoint file and click "Open".

- Wait for a few moments as the PowerPoint content is imported into Sway.

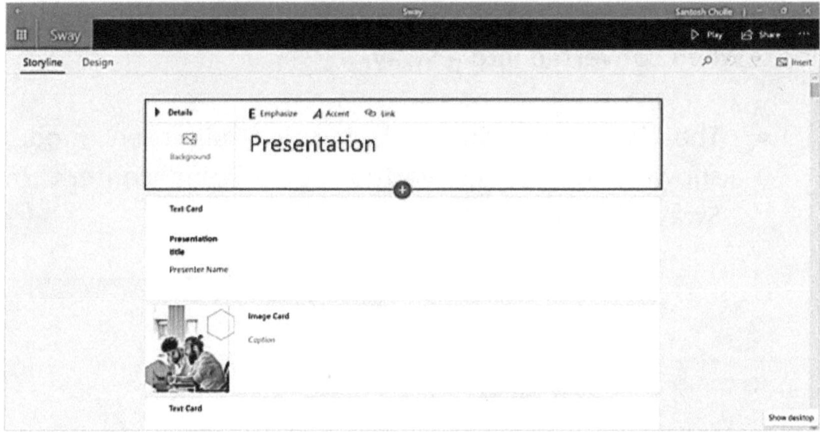

Preview the Sway

To preview your newly created Sway with the imported PowerPoint content, follow these steps:

- In the Sway window, locate the "Play" button in the top right corner.

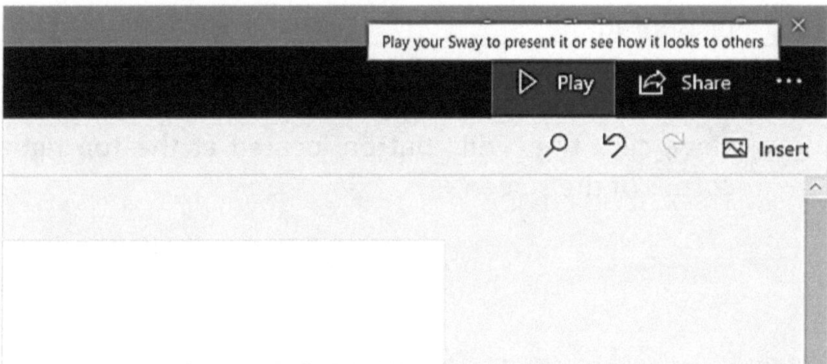

- Click on the "Play" button to launch the preview mode.

You will now be able to see how your PowerPoint presentation looks when converted into a Sway.

- The Sway will start playing in Fullscreen mode, showcasing the converted PowerPoint content in Sway's format.

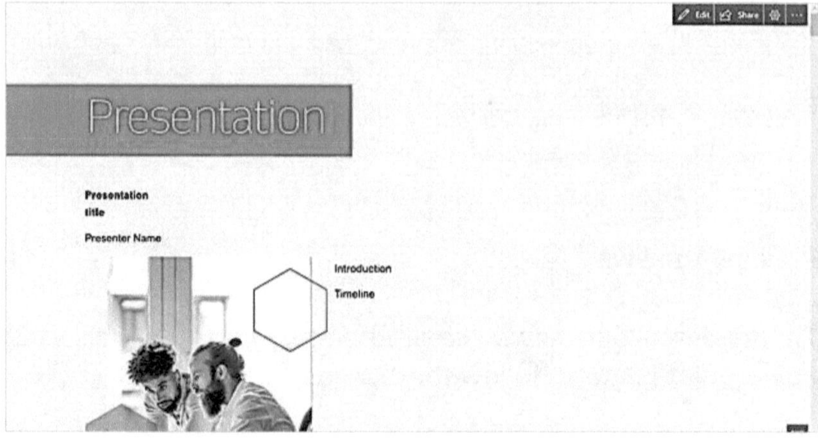

- You can navigate through the Sway using your mouse to see how the PowerPoint content is displayed and presented.

- To exit the Fullscreen mode and return to the Storyline view, click the "Edit" button located at the top right corner of the screen.

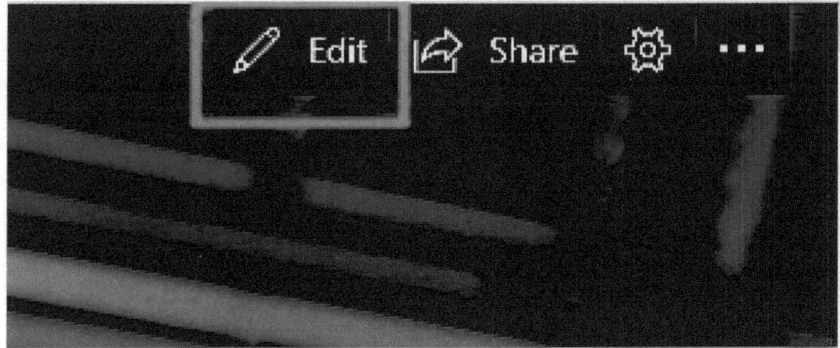

- You will be returned to the Sway storyline to allow you to edit any content as needed I hope this helps to allow you to convert existing PowerPoint presentations into Microsoft Sway.

Shortcut keys

Shortcut Keys	What is does
Ctrl + N	To create a new presentation, press Ctrl + N. This will open a new blank presentation without having to go to the File tab or Office button.
Ctrl + O	To open a presentation, press Ctrl + O. This will display the Open screen in Backstage View, showing recently opened and pinned files.
Ctrl + F12	To open a new presentation via the Open dialog box, press Ctrl + F12. This will bypass the Backstage View area.
Ctrl + S	To save a presentation, press Ctrl + S. If you have not saved the presentation before, you will be prompted to provide a file name and location. If the presentation has been saved previously, it will save any changes made since the last save.
Ctrl + M	To insert a new blank slide, press Ctrl + M. This avoids the need to use the Home tab on the Ribbon.
Ctrl + P	To print the current presentation, press Ctrl + P. This will open the Print Preview window.
Ctrl + Z	To undo an action, press Ctrl + Z. This can be done multiple times to undo multiple actions.

Ctrl + Y	To redo the last action that was undone, press Ctrl + Y.
Ctrl + X	To cut text from its original location, highlight the text and press Ctrl + X.
Ctrl + C	To copy text including the formatting, highlight the text and press Ctrl + C.
Ctrl + V	To paste previously cut or copied text, press Ctrl + V.
Alt + F	To open the File tab, also known as Backstage View, press Alt + F.
Alt	To turn key tips on or off, press Alt.
Alt + Tab	To switch between open programs using thumbnail versions, press Alt + Tab.
Ctrl + Mouse Wheel	To zoom in and out using the wheel on your mouse and the Ctrl key, press Ctrl + Mouse Wheel.
F1	To open the Help system, press F1.
F4	To repeat the last thing done, whether formatting text or deleting an object, press F4.
F12	To perform a Save As regardless of whether the file has been saved before or not, press F12.

Shortcuts used inside a placeholder

Ctrl + B	To apply bold formatting, highlight a word, sentence or bullet point and use Ctrl + B.
Ctrl + I	To apply italics formatting, highlight a word, sentence or bullet point and use Ctrl + I.

Ctrl + U	To apply underline formatting, highlight a word, sentence or bullet point and use Ctrl + U.
Ctrl + A	Use Ctrl + A to select an entire element or object in your presentation. For example, place your cursor inside a placeholder and press Ctrl + A to select ALL of the text included in the placeholder.
Ctrl + L	Use Ctrl + L to left align the selected paragraph inside a placeholder.
Ctrl + R	Use Ctrl + R to right align the selected paragraph inside a placeholder.
Ctrl + E	Use Ctrl + E to centre align the selected paragraph inside a placeholder.
Ctrl + J	Use Ctrl + J to justify align the selected paragraph inside a placeholder.
Ctrl +]	Use Ctrl +] to increase the font size. Keep pressing this combination to keep increasing font size.
Ctrl + [	Use Ctrl + [to decrease the font size. Keep pressing this combination to keep decreasing the size.

Shortcuts used during a presentation

F5	F5 starts the Slide Show mode from the beginning of the presentation.
Shift + F5	Shift + F5 starts the Slide Show mode from the current slide.

Esc	Pressing the Esc key during Slide Show mode exits and returns to the PowerPoint window.
Ctrl + P	Ctrl + P changes the mouse cursor to the Pen tool.
Ctrl + A	Ctrl + A changes the mouse cursor to the Arrow tool.
Ctrl + E	Ctrl + E changes the mouse cursor to the Eraser tool.